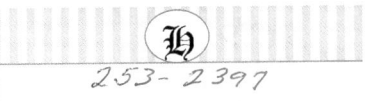

253- 2397

Carlene Harris
1556 Homecoming Ave.
South Jordan, UT 84095-4540

LIFE IS EASY

I Just Decide It's Hard

Ways from the Scriptures to Conquer

Anger
Fear
Worry
Guilt
Perfectionism
Procrastination

LIFE IS EASY*

I Just Decide It's Hard

Ways from the Scriptures to Conquer

Anger
Fear
Worry
Guilt
Perfectionism
Procrastination

by Gary G. Taylor, PhD

CFI
Springville, Utah

* Not really !

ISBN 13: 978-1-59955-066-4

Published by CFI, an imprint of Cedar Fort, Inc., 2373 W. 700 S., Springville, UT, 84663
Distributed by Cedar Fort, Inc. www.cedarfort.com

LIBRARY OF CONGRESS CATALOGING-IN-PUBLICATION DATA

Taylor, Gary G.
   Remedies for emotional headaches / Gary G. Taylor.
      p. cm.
   ISBN 978-1-59955-066-4
   1. Church of Jesus Christ of Latter-Day Saints—Doctrines. 2. Mormon
Church—Doctrines. 3. Emotions—Religious aspects—Mormon Church.
4. Christian life—Mormon authors. I. Title.

   BX8635.3.T39 2007
   248.4'89332—dc22

                    2007026327

Cover design by Nicole Williams
Cover design © 2007 by Lyle Mortimer
Edited and typeset by Kimiko M. Hammari

Printed in the United States of America

10 9 8 7 6 5 4 3 2 1

Printed on acid-free paper

Contents

Introduction

THE SCRIPTURES REMIND US THAT before we came to this world, we shouted for joy at the prospect (see Job 38:7). Now that we are here, it's tempting to wonder what we were so happy about. In mortality, most of us have wonderful life experiences that we wouldn't trade for anything. On the other hand, grief, loss, disappointment, and pain are also a necessary part of the equation. By design, the ride is bumpy and, at times, downright turbulent.

Of the many factors that contribute to a turbulent ride in this life, emotional and mental health problems are among the most significant. It has been estimated that in America alone perhaps one in five, or fifty-six million people, suffer from a debilitating mental illness in some form at some point in their lives. Many of these are severe cases that make normal functioning impossible. Add to this the millions more whose lives are profoundly affected as they care for family and friends with these problems, and it becomes clear that mental illness affects the majority of us in some way.

Then, too, those not directly affected by serious mental illness will still inevitably suffer from at least occasional periods of excessive worry, unnecessary guilt, anger, blue days, and other garden varieties of emotional issues. These "emotional headaches" affect saints and sinners, old and young, all races, and both genders. Though often of relatively minor significance, these episodes still have a significant negative effect on our relationships with others, interfere with our spirituality, and generally lower our quality of life.

In spite of how universal mental and emotional health problems are, it's apparent that some of us have smoother sailing than do others with respect to these issues. Some crash and burn when faced with life events that others handle with relative ease. There are those who handle even very difficult challenges without long-term emotional damage. Many seem to be naturally happy and are rarely stressed, while others seem to be negative and irritable by nature. Why is that? Why do some seem to have much better mental and emotional health than others? Is it explained by personality or some innate ability? Is it purely the result of genetic inheritance, or does it result from a set of skills that anyone can develop? Can we learn to manage our emotional life and improve our mental health?

Unfortunately, it's not yet possible to answer questions like these definitively from the standpoint of medical science. Even though there have been many exciting discoveries in recent years, the functioning of the brain is so marvelously complex that there remain more questions than answers about its specific operation. It seems clear, however, that mental illness is somehow related to problems in brain function or structure. It seems to follow that normal emotional ups and downs are affected by similar processes. It makes sense to think of a continuum with life-threatening depression or paralyzing anxiety disorders at one end, blue days or periods of unusual anxiety that we all experience a little further along the continuum, and happiness and joy at the other end. Yet how points along this continuum connect and the exact physiological processes involved remain largely a mystery.

In spite of this mystery, there is solid evidence that certain interventions can move us toward the positive end of the mental health continuum. For instance, an ever increasing number of medications have led many who suffer from mental illness to lead normal lives again. "Talk therapy" has proven to be even more effective in some cases. Various clinical approaches in which therapists help clients identify and correct problems in how they think have, in some instances, been shown to relieve symptoms of even serious mental illness. These approaches have also proven to be effective in helping individuals better manage the ordinary emotional upset that we all experience.

The success of non-medical therapies demonstrates what we think is an important factor in the equation. Since what we think is largely under conscious control, there must be steps we can take to improve our mental and emotional health. The skills involved may come more naturally to some than to others, and they may not even be possible in certain cases of serious mental illness. In those instances, medication or other medical interventions may be necessary in order to restore normal brain function before we can successfully control what we think. But the bottom line is that virtually all of us can improve our mental and emotional health.

This fact fits nicely with the message of scripture that suggests that happiness and joy are the result of thinking and living righteously. This is true both with respect to eternal happiness and joy (see Alma 3:26) and to happiness in this life (see 4 Nephi 1:15–16). The scriptures also provide specific suggestions about how to improve our emotional and mental health. The good news is that God's plan of happiness comes complete with a set of emotional shock absorbers that can help us smooth out the bumps in life.

In July of 1838, the Prophet Joseph Smith was at an extremely low point in his life and was reminded of some of these tools. Joseph had been incarcerated in Liberty Jail for several months. Conditions in the jail were horrible and constituted cruel and unusual punishment by any reasonable standard. Worse, Joseph and his associates had been falsely accused, which made their personal suffering all the more difficult to accept. But no doubt the biggest problem he faced came from the reports Joseph received regarding the struggles of family, friends, and associates. Many had been driven from their homes in Missouri under desperate conditions, and a number had died as a result of violent persecution while Joseph was incarcerated and unable to do anything directly to help them.

It was under these extreme conditions that Joseph pled with God for relief. In section 121 of the Doctrine and Covenants we read excerpts from that heartrending prayer: "O God, where art thou? And where is the pavilion that covereth thy hiding place? How long shall thy hand be stayed, and thine eye, yea thy pure eye, behold from the eternal heavens the wrongs of thy people and of thy servants, and thine ear be penetrated with their cries?" (vv. 1–2). Joseph then went on to request that the Lord defend the Saints and destroy their enemies: "Let thine anger be kindled against our enemies; and, in the fury of thine heart, with thy sword avenge us of our wrongs" (v. 5).

Students of history know that this prayer was not answered in the way that Joseph requested. In the Lord's wisdom, events were allowed to play out in Missouri, and Zion was not redeemed at that time. Instead, God gave Joseph tools that he and others could use to make their burden lighter and to help them patiently endure their plight. These tools, which are described in the Doctrine and Covenants beginning in verse 7 of section 121, are universally applicable. They will help each of us as we face challenges in the same way that they undoubtedly helped Joseph.

The first helpful comment to Joseph came in the Lord's salutation, "My son, peace be unto thy soul" (D&C 121:7). No matter what we face, it helps immensely to remember who we are. Even though we may suffer from a mental illness or some other form of adversity, it helps to remember that we are literally children of God. It helps to remember that He knows us by name and He knows what we are experiencing. When events combine against us and our best efforts don't seem to be enough to save the day, it's comforting to remember that God is in charge and those committed to following the Lord will ultimately prevail (3 Nephi 24:14–18).

Next, Joseph was given a very useful piece of advice. He was reminded that "[his] adversity and [his] afflictions [would] be but a small moment" (D&C 121:7). Research indicates that those who handle difficulties in life well tend to think of their problems as temporary. They tend to think things like, "I don't like this, but I know it's temporary. I'm going to get through this. It's bad now, but things will get better." Conversely, those who don't handle problems well tend to think that there is no end to their struggle. They think things like, "I'll never recover from this. Life is over for me. I'm never going to be happy again." It doesn't take a genius to see the implication of thinking in these different ways. Problems are a lot more painful and difficult to bear if we fail to remember that they are temporary.

The next tool is given in verse 8. Here the Lord pointed Joseph to the ultimate achievement possible: "And then, if thou endure it well, God shall exalt thee on high; thou shalt triumph over all thy foes." The pain of the moment has meaning when we see its connection to our ultimate goal. A vision of Joseph's eternal future would have made the problems in the moment shrink in significance. A vision of Joseph's eternal future would have put his suffering in context and given it purpose. The same applies to those suffering the effects of significant emotional distress in any of its forms.

In verse 9 Joseph is reminded that even in the middle of serious trouble, not everything in his life was bad: "Thy friends do stand by thee and they shall hail thee again with warm hearts and friendly hands." Research indicates that along with thinking of problems as being temporary, those who handle problems well think of their troubles as limited in scope. Those who handle difficulties poorly think of their problems as pervasive. They think things like, "My life is totally ruined. Nothing is working out for me. Everything is messed up." The truth is that there are always positive aspects to our lives, even during the worst of times. Those who focus on the positives inevitably enjoy better mental health and less emotional distress than those who focus on the negatives.

In verse 10 Joseph is asked to compare his life to someone who suffered even more deeply: "Thou art not yet as Job; thy friends do not contend against thee, neither charge thee with transgression, as they did Job." Someone has said that if we faced a pile of all the troubles in the world and were given a choice between taking an equal share from the pile or keeping the problems we have at the moment, we would all decide to keep our existing problems. That may or may not be true, but it certainly helps to understand that our suffering has limits and that others have endured as much or more than we have. It also helps to remember that Christ is the ultimate example in this regard. Having suffered infinitely more than any of us ever could or would, Christ understands perfectly our pain and trials. He also understands our limits and has promised assistance when the load is too heavy for us to bear (see 1 Corinthians 10:14; D&C 64:20). *V. 13*

Finally, in verses 11 through 33 of section 121, the Lord gives Joseph a view of the sad state of those who fight against righteousness. Based on this understanding, there was no need for Joseph to spend energy seeking justice for the Saints. He could stop worrying about the things he couldn't control and leave all such matters to the Lord. Doing so would have removed a great deal of frustration and fear, thus allowing Joseph to experience relative peace in the midst of continued provocation and turmoil.

The advice given to Joseph at this difficult time and the tools offered are both practical and universal. The same steps can help any of us improve our emotional and mental health. As an example, consider Mary, who is a struggling single mother of five children. Life was basically good for Mary until the day her former husband announced that he was in love with someone else and that he was filing for divorce. Since that painful announcement, Mary's emotions have been a tangle of anger, guilt, fear, and self-doubt. Her health has suffered, and her relationships with her children and others have become strained. Mary doesn't have enough money to meet her family's needs, and she doesn't have the time or energy to satisfy the demands of home and work. She would much prefer being a full-time mother, but she is forced to work outside of the home in a job she doesn't enjoy.

The tools outlined above given to the Prophet Joseph in the Liberty Jail can significantly lighten Mary's burden as they did Joseph's. For one thing, she needs to regularly focus on the fact that she is God's daughter with an eternal destiny. This will take some effort on the days when the babysitter doesn't show up, the car refuses to start, or she doesn't have money to pay the bills. But whenever she catches the vision of who she is and where she is headed, no trouble she faces will seem that important. It's a little like what happens to us emotionally at a time in our life when nothing seems to be going right until something wonderful happens. The problems that so upset us remain the same, but our good fortune nullifies their emotional consequence. When we focus on our good fortune, problems are just not that big of a deal. Given Christ's gift and the resulting eternal possibilities, all of us are most fortunate—no matter the degree of pain in the moment.

A second tool is to remember that problems are temporary. Mary needs to keep repeating, "This is miserable, but I know it's temporary. I'm going to get through this. I'm going to be happy again." And, of course, that's true. Mary may not see the end to some of her problems from her current vantage point, but she can trust that they will end in due time. Mary can also count on help along the way. As a matter of fact, Mary had been greatly distraught a number of times thinking how she couldn't possibly deal with some new wrinkle in her life—like the time she got sick and assumed that she would not be able to keep her job or pay her medical bills. But somehow those situations never ended up being the disaster they seemed to be at first, and somehow there was always ultimately a way to manage the problem.

According to the third suggestion provided in section 121, Mary should focus on the eternal blessings that have been promised. Life for Mary isn't fair in the short-term. She did nothing to justify her former husband's failure to honor his covenants. The ensuing money problems and other difficulties she faces are undeserved. Even more disturbing, in a way, is that life for Mary's former husband is going pretty well. He has a companion he enjoys, more discretionary income, and more opportunities. In light of this reality, Mary needs to remember that as she stays the course ("if thou endure it well"), her blessings will far exceed anything she can imagine. Likewise, her former husband will also reap the rewards of his poor choices.

As the prophet Malachi pointed out, "Now we call the proud happy; yea, they that work wickedness are set up; yea they that tempt God are even delivered" (Malachi 3:15). But in the end, justice will be served and everyone rewarded according to merit. That's when we need to decide whether serving the Lord is worthwhile, not during the heat of the mortal battle. "Then shall ye return, and discern between the righteous and the wicked, between him that serveth God and him that serveth him not" (Malachi 3:18). This perspective is important for Mary as she tries to forgive her former husband and deal with the unfairness of her *temporary* situation. She can leave all of this with the Lord and trust that everything will be fine at the end of the day.

Interestingly, at some level, Mary understood this truth all along, but that knowledge didn't help her very much. When asked during a counseling session if she would trade places with her husband at the moment, she said, "Definitely not!" Even if she could snap her fingers and have a great husband, a good job, and more discretionary income, she wouldn't do it if it meant also accepting the eternal consequences associated with her former husband's choices. The reason this understanding wasn't helping Mary emotionally probably amounts to the simple fact that she wasn't focusing on it. Emotions are affected by what we are thinking, consciously or subconsciously, *at the moment*. A knowledge of truth won't help if, in spite of that knowledge, we think negative, self-centered, and self-defeating thoughts. A knowledge of the truth can also get lost if our habits of thought, general attitudes, or programmed thinking (known as schemas, as talked about later) are unhealthy.

Another tool from section 121 that would help is for Mary to focus on the positives in her life. The temptation is for her to think that her life is a total mess and everything is ruined. In fact, many of the good things in her life continue in spite of the divorce. This has been no doubt a gut-wrenching experience for Mary, but this catastrophic event didn't negate everything good in her life. Her faith in God continues, along with her relationship with her children and extended family and friends. Mary's talents and abilities are not negated. Future opportunities in this life and eternal potential continue. It may seem at times like her life is ruined, but that simply isn't true. It is true, however, that the level of pain she experiences is affected by how she views her situation. Following the guidelines from section 121 outlined previously will definitely help.

More detail will be given in later chapters regarding how Mary can practically apply these and other suggestions found in scripture. As she does so, the emotional pain in her situation will be significantly reduced and her mental health will improve. This is also true even in cases of serious mental illness. Situations like the one Mary faces can trigger an episode of major depression in those genetically or otherwise predisposed. In that case, an individual is consumed by negative thoughts and is not amenable to cheering up. Those suffering from major depression experience a clinically significant impairment of social, occupational, and personal functioning and an intense pain that pretty much has to be experienced to be understood. But even those experiencing such profound symptoms can be helped by applying the principles taught in scripture.

I have long noticed an interesting phenomenon when providing therapy to individuals who are extremely depressed or anxious. Their moods are dramatic in intensity but also in variability. They can be suffering an intense pain one moment and joking or feeling more at peace at another—*all depending on what they are thinking at the moment.* Even though nothing has been done to directly change their body chemistry or brain function, and even though the life difficulties they face have not changed, they have moments of peace or positive reality.

Of course, a depressed or anxious mood may quickly return. It usually takes multiple therapy sessions, sometimes medication, and a person's effort over time before lasting change occurs. But the fact that a client's mood improves even temporarily reinforces two points made earlier. First, it suggests that emotions are controlled, at least to some extent, by what we think. Second, it suggests that even profoundly unhappy or anxious people can have some control over what they think. The trick seems to lie in breaking old habits and developing the skill involved in managing one's thoughts. It is *not* possible to control a mood simply by wishing it away or trying to control it directly. Deciding "I'm not going to be depressed today" isn't going to do much good if the individual continues to think depressing, counterproductive things. But it is possible to change specific thoughts, frames of reference, and even habits of thought. Doing so can, in turn, over time (but even sometimes immediately and dramatically) improve moods.

In short, we can use our minds to process events differently and to better manage emotion—which can have immediate but also long-range benefits. Researchers at the UCLA School of Medicine, using positron emission tomography (PET), have demonstrated physical changes in the brain chemistry resulting simply from cognitive behavioral therapy; that is, where changes in thinking have occurred without any medication. In his book *The Mind and the Brain: Neuroplasticity and the Power of Mental Force* (Regan Books, 2002), Dr. Jeffrey M. Schwartz points to these and other studies suggesting that the brain can be "rewired" or reshaped when we make substantive changes in our thinking. Based on this research, it looks possible to change the actual function of our brains as we make willful choices to think more productively.

This is an exciting possibility that fits nicely with the concepts of free will and moral agency, which are clearly taught in scripture. Scripture also, of course, provides excellent direction regarding the specifics of what and how we should think in order to manage ourselves productively. In the remaining chapters, the suggestions from scripture outlined above, along with a number of others, will be reviewed in terms of how they impact our emotional and mental health.

In the Book of Mormon we read, "And now, my sons, remember, remember that it is upon the rock of our Redeemer, who is Christ, the Son of God, that ye must build your foundation; that when the devil shall send forth his mighty winds, yea, his shafts in the whirlwind, yea, when all his hail and his mighty storm shall beat upon you, it shall have no power over you to drag you down to the gulf of misery and endless wo, because of the rock upon which ye are built, which is a sure foundation, a foundation whereon if men build they cannot fall" (Helaman 5:12).

As we build our emotional foundation on the teachings of Christ, and as we attempt to live our lives following His example, we will be doing those things upon which good emotional and mental health depends. We will be doing those things that help us heal from the effects of our individual biological and environmental heritage. As a result, we will be able to experience greater happiness and joy even as we encounter the difficulties of mortality. The following chapters discuss how this can work in our lives from a practical standpoint.

CHAPTER

1 Guilt can be a blessing or a curse

THE SCRIPTURES TEACH THAT GUILT is a necessary and useful emotion. Paul reminds us that guilt—which he calls godly sorrow—"worketh repentance to salvation" (2 Corinthians 7:10). Guilt can be thought of as the moral equivalent of physical pain. If the body is functioning properly, putting a hand on a hot stove hurts. The pain is an effective warning that inevitable tissue damage will result if your hand is not removed from the stove. Guilt, likewise, is a painful emotion that can signal the need to remove yourself from conduct that will inevitably lead to emotional or spiritual damage.

One excellent example of this in scripture is the story of Zeezrom, which begins in chapter 11 of Alma in the Book of Mormon. Zeezrom proved to be quite effective in using deception and sophistry in turning people against the prophets and away from the truth. In a confrontation with the prophet Alma, however, Zeezrom became convinced that he was fighting against God. With that understanding, he began to "tremble under a consciousness of his guilt" (Alma 12:1). Later, the guilt he experienced was so extreme that he became physically ill. "And also Zeezrom lay sick at Sidom, with a burning fever, which was caused by the great tribulations of his mind on account of his wickedness" (Alma 15:3).

The prophet Alma visited Zeezrom in his troubled state and promised that he could be healed if he believed in the redemption of Christ. Zeezrom confirmed his belief, and Alma prayed, "Oh Lord our God, have mercy on this man, and heal him according to his faith which is in Christ." And then "when Alma had said these words, Zeezrom leaped

1

upon his feet, and began to walk; and this was done to the great astonishment of all the people" (Alma 15:10–11).

This is a powerful story of guilt and redemption. Guilt, the oppressive awareness of having sinned, resulted in emotional turmoil within Zeezrom and eventually in physical illness. The good news is that the guilt he experienced softened his soul and led Zeezrom to repentance. Then, after repentance, both the physical and emotional manifestations of guilt were swept away through acceptance of the Atonement of Jesus Christ.

Of course, Zeezrom experienced guilt only after coming to understand the extent of his sin. Like all of us, Zeezrom came into the world preprogrammed with a conscience that gave him a basic knowledge of right and wrong (see D&C 84:46). Like many of us, Zeezrom was able to ignore his native conscience and to anesthetize guilt. In 1 Timothy the Apostle Paul likens this process to "having [our] conscience seared with a hot iron" (1 Timothy 4:2). By ignoring guilt long enough, a person eventually gets to a place where he is "past feeling" (Ephesians 4:19). Presumably Zeezrom knew early on that he was on the wrong path, but the thrill of his success and the attention he got in his community led him to convince himself that he was doing just fine. Once convinced, guilt was suppressed and not allowed to surface.

This lasted until the power of Alma's testimony crashed through the defenses against truth that Zeezrom had constructed in his mind. At that point, he was immersed in guilt—which is apparently an inevitable experience for those who are unrepentant. As King Benjamin indicated, "Therefore if that man repenteth not, and remaineth and dieth an enemy to God, the demands of justice do awaken his immortal soul to a lively sense of his own guilt, which doth cause him to shrink from the presence of the Lord, and doth fill his breast with guilt, and pain, and anguish, which is like an unquenchable fire, whose flame ascendeth up forever and ever" (Mosiah 2:38). According to King Benjamin, even if we put it off in this life, we will inevitably experience the guilt that naturally follows an awareness of our sins. For that reason, the sooner we recognize guilt and let it lead us to repentance, the better.

All of this suggests that guilt is an inevitable, important, and useful tool in our spiritual progress. But as helpful and necessary as it is, it's also true that guilt can be a detriment in our lives if it is taken too far, or if it is misapplied in some way. As discussed in detail later, this happens when we feel guilty even after repentance or when we feel guilty about something for which we are not responsible. Unnecessary guilt occurs when we feel excessive sorrow about essentially normal behavior or for something that isn't even a moral issue. Unfortunately, those who feel guilty for no good reason may suffer as intensely as those who feel guilty with cause. Unnecessary guilt results in emotional turmoil, contributes to poor mental health, and robs us of motivation to improve ourselves. This fact has led some mental health experts to unwisely suggest that we try to eliminate all guilt from our lives. That would be a classic example of throwing the baby out with the bath water. Rather than eliminate guilt, we need to use it to help us develop our spiritual potential. At the same time, there is no reason to fall victim to unnecessary guilt.

In effect, we need to decide when guilt is and is not appropriate and then act accordingly. A general rule of thumb in making this distinction is found in scripture. It is the test suggested by Moroni in chapter 7 of the book of Moroni:

> For behold, the Spirit of Christ is given to every man, that he may know good from evil; wherefore, I show unto you the way to judge; for every thing which inviteth to do good, and to persuade to believe in Christ, is sent forth by the power and gift of Christ; wherefore ye may know with a perfect knowledge it is of God. But whatsoever thing persuadeth men to do evil, and believe not in Christ, and deny him, and serve not God, then ye may know with a perfect knowledge it is of the devil; for after this manner doth the devil work, for he persuadeth no man to do good, no, not one; neither do his angels; neither do they who subject themselves unto him. (Moroni 7:16–17)

Sometimes guilt becomes so intense and misplaced that it is counter-motivating. It leads an individual to self-doubt and lose faith. Rather than encouraging repentance, it leads a person to give up. Such guilt denies the power of the Atonement and the place of mercy in the eternal plan. Based on Moroni's test, the author of such guilt is certainly not God.

In addition to this general rule, four additional criteria can help distinguish between healthy and unnecessary guilt. All four criteria are compatible with principles taught in scripture.

Guilt is unnecessary after we have repented

The prophet Alma described how guilt, repentance, and the Atonement function ideally in our lives when he described his own experience to his son Helaman. Alma sinned grievously in his younger days, for which at one point he suffered intense guilt. He told Helaman, "I was racked with eternal torment, for my soul was harrowed up to the greatest degree and racked with all my sins. Yea, I did remember all my sins and iniquities, for which I was tormented with the pains of hell; yea, I saw that I had rebelled against my God, and that I had not kept his holy commandments" (Alma 36:13–14).

At some point through this period of despair, Alma began to focus his mind on the principle of the Atonement and the mercy available through Jesus Christ. He said, "And now, behold, when I thought this, I could remember my pains no more; yea, I was harrowed up by the memory of my sins no more. And oh, what joy, and what marvelous light I did behold; yea, my soul was filled with joy as exceeding as was my pain!" (Alma 36:19–20).

Guilt can lead to repentance, but it is then no longer necessary—at least, not with respect to the behavior we have put behind us. Unfortunately, some keep the guilt going and don't complete the cycle. The relief and joy described by Alma then elude them. Sandra is an example. Sandra was a child of promise raised in an active LDS home with numerous temporal and spiritual blessings. As a youth she was extremely talented, highly intelligent, and spiritually motivated. But at some point she took the wrong path. She began to experiment with drugs, her grades dropped, and she became sexually active. She felt so horrible about herself that she accepted a marriage proposal early out of high school from someone with a drug addiction, no job, no prospects, and a temper problem.

After several years she found herself with a child, no husband, no advanced education, and estranged from the Church. She was still extremely talented, highly intelligent, and spiritually motivated, but the intense guilt she felt led her to doubt herself. She believed that she had lost all opportunity. She believed that she could never be accepted back into the Church or achieve her educational goals. She also assumed that the kind of man that she would consider marrying would never be interested in her. In fact, she sabotaged every promising social opportunity. For instance, she was very interested in one ideal marriage candidate and he was equally interested in her, but she simply quit returning his calls. She wasn't aware of it at the time, but she did so to protect herself. She was operating on the assumption that this fellow could not possibly love and accept her once he knew the truth about her background. She subconsciously decided that it was therefore best to cut off the relationship before she became too emotionally involved.

In Sandra's case, the guilt she felt motivated her to give up drugs and to generally get her life in order. So motivated, she filed for divorce to protect both herself and her daughter from abuse. She got a good job and worked hard at being a good mother. She sacrificed her own needs in order to take care of various responsibilities, but she was not happy. And she was afraid to return to full activity in the Church or to pursue educational and social opportunities. She had little self-confidence.

The day was saved for Sandra when she, like Alma, caught a vision of the power of the Atonement and the prophet Isaiah's words: "Though your sins be as scarlet, they shall be as white as snow" (Isaiah 1:18). Sandra had long known this scripture and had theoretically understood the power of the Atonement. But at some point the Atonement became personal. She moved from a theoretical belief to a knowledge that God would forgive *her*. She decided that if God could forgive her, then others could too, and she could forgive herself. All of her eternal potential remained. All of her important goals in this life were still open. Even the man of her dreams could accept, love, and respect her—assuming she could accept, love, and respect herself. Through Christ, every important thing in her life was still possible.

Once she focused on her Savior's gift rather than on her sin, she moved past guilt and began to experience self-confidence and joy. She was able to feel good about herself because of the positive changes she had made. She became confident about her future, thanks to her faith in the Atonement. This faith motivated her to get back to church and to complete the process of putting her life back fully on track. None of this would have happened if she had continued to be mired in guilt. Again, guilt served an important and necessary function in Sandra's life up to the point of her solid efforts to repent, but it became an unhealthy and unnecessary problem when taken too far.

As another example of unnecessary guilt, this time regarding a more mundane sin, consider Brad's story. Brad had an honesty problem much of his life. He would deny responsibility for mistakes and even subtly lay the blame on others when he could get away with it. He regularly did things like call in sick in order to extend a vacation or just to get a day off. He would glibly lie about his age or residence in order to get a discount at various places. In general, he would fudge on the truth whenever it suited his purposes in order to manipulate outcomes and take advantage of situations. All of these indiscretions were rationalized as minor sins. After all, he wasn't a thief, and he didn't break the law. In fact, he thought of himself as being rather clever, and he thought of those who had a problem with the kind of things he did as being foolish and morally uptight.

Over time, however, Brad's level of morality evolved. He began to understand that his dishonest behavior, even though relatively minor, was inappropriate. He wanted to eventually be part of a celestial world, and he began to realize that *everyone* in such a world would need to be *absolutely* trustworthy. He came to understand that the least degree of evil cannot be tolerated in the presence of God (see D&C 1:31), not because God is intolerant but because it would corrupt an otherwise perfect world. The celestial kingdom would cease to be celestial.

With this understanding, Brad started to feel guilty about behavior in which he had casually and even comfortably participated. This guilt was healthy, and it motivated him to make changes. Sometimes he wouldn't catch himself until after the fact, but he did recognize and largely eliminate all dishonest behavior in his life. Even so, he didn't lose the temptation. He still recognized opportunities to take advantage of situations, and he still had a desire to do so. In some cases, it took considerable effort to make the right decision. This fact caused him to doubt himself and led him to discount the progress he had made. That aspect of his guilt was not healthy. It caused him unnecessary discomfort and at times led him to wonder, "Why bother?"

This unhealthy aspect to Brad's guilt was related, in part, to his interpretation of a comment made by Mosiah in the Book of Mormon. The people of Mosiah were touched by the Spirit and had a mighty change in their hearts. From that point they had "no more disposition to do evil, but to do good continually" (Mosiah 5:2). Even though he no longer acted on the desire, Brad still thought about taking advantage of others. In his interpretation, that meant that a disposition to evil remained and his repentance was therefore incomplete.

Brad was also aware of instances in scripture in which people are condemned for their thoughts (see Matthew 5:28; 15:18–20). In fact, in Matthew 5:28 the Lord is particularly forceful in pointing out that "whosoever looketh on a woman to lust after her hath committed adultery with her already in his heart." Brad continued to have dishonest thoughts and worried that he would be condemned by those thoughts.

His concern was similar to a young missionary who is troubled by sexual thoughts that come into his mind at times. The missionary doesn't do things that invite those thoughts into his mind. He doesn't dwell on them or act on them, but there they are. Or as another example, a homosexual puts great effort into successfully avoiding homosexual behavior but continues to have homosexual desire. Are these examples of what the Savior is condemning in the scripture cited above? We must interpret our personal situation individually, but it would seem that the Lord is condemning focused rather than stray or random thoughts. Some invite sexual or other immoral thoughts into their mind and then dwell and expand upon them once they enter. They find pleasure in thinking evil and make no attempt to deny such thoughts. This kind of thinking needs to be repented of, whether it's associated with explicit immoral behavior or not. Random thought or day-to-day temptations that come into our minds from whatever source, no matter how persistent, do not seem to be in the same category.

If the standard is thought of in this way, Brad can feel good about the changes he has made in eliminating dishonest behavior from his life. There is no need to feel guilty about the fact that temptations still come into his mind. The missionary and the homosexual need to continue to put immoral thoughts out of their minds and avoid dwelling on them, but there is no reason to feel guilty about the fact that those thoughts come unbidden from time to time. Temptation appears to be a natural and inevitable part of life. Even Jesus was visited by the tempter (see Matthew 4). No doubt we do lose an inclination to evil over time as we persist in doing good, but perhaps we don't need to wait for that to happen completely before we forgive ourselves and feel good about efforts to repent and improve our lives.

It's unnecessary to feel guilty about things we can't control

Agency, the power to direct our lives as we choose, is one of the foundation principles of the gospel. David O. McKay once observed, "Next to the bestowal of life itself, the right to direct that life is God's greatest gift to man."[1] But, of course, with that agency comes responsibility. As much as we might like to blame someone or something else at times, the fact that we have agency makes us solely responsible for our mistakes. By the same token, the fact that everyone has agency means that we are *not* responsible for the mistakes of others. Yet all too often, that is exactly what we feel.

This is particularly true of parents who have children that make disappointing choices. Latter-day Saint parents generally understand the importance of their role, and they believe strongly in the now famous statement by President David O. McKay: "No success in life can compensate for failure in the home."[2] Most Latter-day Saint parents also take seriously the words of the Lord in D&C 68:25: "And again, inasmuch as parents have children in Zion, or in any of her stakes which are organized, that teach them not to understand the doctrine of repentance, faith in Christ the Son of the living God, and baptism and the gift of the Holy Ghost by the laying on of the hands, when eight years old, the sin be upon the heads of the parents."

The problem is that those who understand the importance of their role as parents sometimes take that responsibility too far. All parents are responsible to teach their children and to do what they can to help them make good choices, but they cannot force their children to make the right decisions. Therefore, parents are responsible for their own choices with respect to their children, but they are not responsible for the choices their children make. Christ, the Master Teacher, was responsible while here on earth to live and teach the truth, which He did perfectly. He was not responsible for the fact that so many who heard His teaching refused to accept it.

Brother and Sister Adams are examples of parents who have taken their sense of responsibility too far. They are great parents—not perfect, but great. Lola Adams is particularly invested in her children. She holds advanced degrees and might have had an exciting career, but she opted to stay home and raise her five children. Over the years, both parents have helped their children with schoolwork, tried to hold consistent family home evenings, taken their children to church, enrolled them in numerous activities, and generally done what they could to teach their children correct principles by both precept and example.

In spite of their efforts, two of their children have so far taken a different path. One of their daughters has been in and out of numerous immoral and destructive relationships with men, and she will have nothing to do with the Church. One of their sons has become addicted to methamphetamines and has also lost interest in his religion. He has not been able to hold a job consistently, and he has had problems with the law resulting in jail time on two separate occasions.

Mom and Dad are understandably disappointed and concerned about the mistakes these children have made. Unfortunately, they also feel guilty. In spite of all their effort, they feel like failures as parents.

The guilt they feel centers on a common but inaccurate conclusion. They assume that their children's problems provide *prima facie* evidence of their failure. "We must have done something wrong, or our kids wouldn't have these problems." Wrong! By this standard Adam and Eve were failures as parents. After all, one son murdered another. Lehi and Sariah must have also been failures since several of their children were rebellious and exceptionally wicked. Even our eternal parents fail by this standard. As perfect as they are, one third of their children contradicted their will and were forever cast out (see Revelation 12:4).

The truth seems clear. Parents err if they judge their success on the basis of how their children turn out. Some parents are failures even though their children turn out well. All of us know individuals who were neglected and abused as children but who overcame that poor start and ended up living successful lives. Others, like the Adamses, are successful parents even though their children fail in some way. A great deal of unnecessary pain can be avoided if parents understand this fact.

In the case of Lola Adams, for example, her unnecessary guilt led to significant problems. Being genetically predisposed to clinical depression, obsessive thoughts of her "failure" triggered several episodes of major depression. During those periods, Lola suffered intense pain and, of course, was not able to function effectively in her home, social life, or church responsibilities. At several points her condition was life threatening.

Beyond triggering depression, Lola's guilt led to other problems as well. Feeling responsible for their behavior led Lola to be generally manipulative and controlling with her children. Those traits naturally put her children off and strained her relationship with them. Her need to control the situation also led to many arguments with her husband when he didn't agree with Lola on some point.

In short, the guilt that Lola experienced was most destructive—and totally unnecessary. The same thing can happen any time we feel guilty about something over which we have no control. Perhaps we feel guilty for a marriage that failed in spite of our best effort to save it. We might be in charge of a social event and feel guilty when it fails in spite of our solid effort to make it a success. Others feel guilty when they get sick or don't recover quickly, thinking that they lack faith or strength of character. This is particularly common in cases of emotional or mental illness. It's so easy to blame ourselves rather than understand that the problem is largely beyond our control. At a more mundane level, as discussed next, it's also unnecessary to feel guilty for a mistake we make due to temporary lapses that are a natural part of the human condition.

Guilt about ordinary imperfections is unnecessary

Some things are just part of the human condition. Not long ago I volunteered to be an election judge in our local precinct. I was assigned to greet voters and look them up in the official voter register before ballots were issued. The problem is that I have a relatively poor memory for names, and a good percentage of those who came to vote were neighbors and members of my ward and stake who I see regularly and should know by name. True to form, especially with the pressure of people in line, I just couldn't remember some of their names. This was more or less embarrassing depending on how well I knew the person; but all in all, it was an uncomfortable situation.

This kind of thing happens regularly to most of us. We can't remember something that we should, we mishandle social situations, we make innocent mistakes in judgment, or we reveal our human imperfections in any number of other ways. Apologies are obviously in order when we hurt others. It also makes sense to learn from mistakes and do our best to avoid them. For example, next time I volunteer as an election judge, I plan to take some time beforehand reviewing names from ward and stake lists. On the other hand, it does no good to feel guilty. If I got carried away feeling guilty after the election judge experience, I might be tempted to avoid serving next time. Or perhaps I might feel so bad about forgetting a particular person's name that I end up avoiding that person in the future or otherwise acting uncomfortable around him. I might develop sufficient self-doubt that I become generally awkward in social situations. In that case, peace of mind would be destroyed and self-confidence weakened, at least temporarily.

The same thing can happen when we feel guilty about not being perfect in some way. Many homemakers feel unnecessary guilt if their house is not spotless or if their kids don't look perfect when they go to church or school. In spite of considerable effort to lose pounds, many people feel guilty about their weight. Some feel great guilt if they forget a birthday or say something embarrassing in public. As discussed in some detail in the next chapter, no one is perfect in this life; nor do we need to be. Ironically, expecting perfection in ourselves actually holds us back in our pursuit of perfection, and it's also upsetting to our emotional and mental health.

It's unnecessary to feel guilty about nonmoral issues

Feeling guilty about essentially nonmoral issues is a common problem. Julie had this habit in spades, and it seriously impacted her emotional and mental health. Julie suffered from intense joint pain to the extent that she was no longer able to work at her job as an airline reservation specialist, nor could she do much around the house. She went from doctor to doctor and tried various medications with little positive effect. Various explanations for her condition didn't pan out, and she was left with a serious problem for which there was no clear diagnosis and no cure.

Julie is a person of faith and prayed long and hard for a cure. She received several priesthood blessings, and her family fasted for her. In spite of all this, when I met her, this condition had been with her for months. There was still no viable diagnosis, and she was hurting more than ever. By this time, she was also suffering from depression and anxiety. To a large extent, the depression and anxiety were related to the fact that she was unnecessarily feeling an overwhelming guilt because of her condition.

She thought that she was weak. She would say things like, "I should go to work, or at least do more things around the house," even though her condition made many things impossible to do and she suffered greatly whenever she exerted herself too much. She assumed her faith was weak. "If I had sufficient faith, I know I would be healed." She thought she was a terrible wife and mother. "I'm good for nothing. My kids and husband would be so much better off without me and my problems dragging them down." She thought that she made no contribution to the world. "I'm not accomplishing anything. My life is a mess." Finally, she began to think that her problems would never be solved. "I'm never going to feel normal again. For some reason, God must want me to suffer."

It's not surprising that this kind of thinking was depressing and made Julie anxious. It was also unnecessary. As suggested earlier, Julie was not responsible for her poor health. Of course, technically, she was responsible for how she thought about her problem—a root issue in the depression and anxiety she experienced—but even here, she didn't have control without help. First, she didn't really understand the power she had to control her thinking. It all seemed pretty automatic. Further, much of what she thought was below awareness. She became aware of this thinking and understood how to change it only after third party intervention. Up to that point, she was not in control because she didn't have the necessary information to effect change—a common human condition.

But even if she was responsible in some way for her plight, which she was not, none of what she felt guilty about involved moral issues. Getting sick is no fun and is something we try to avoid, but it's obviously not immoral. Good people get sick, and being ill does not make someone a bad person (see John 9:1–3). The limits on what Julie could do at work and around the house because of her ailment were disappointing, but these limits by no means qualified as sin. Julie was still eligible for a temple recommend whether she did the laundry or not. The limits on what she could do were simply a fact of her situation, not right or wrong. Even her supposed lack of faith to be healed was not a moral issue.

First of all, people are sometimes not healed even when they have great faith. As an example, the Apostle Paul, obviously a person of great faith, was not healed in spite of praying earnestly three times for relief from his "thorn in the flesh." Rather than healing him, the Lord told Paul, "My grace is sufficient for thee; for my strength is made perfect in weakness" (2 Corinthians 12:7–9). Paul was not healed for reasons known to the Lord, not because of a lack of faith on Paul's part. Likewise, the fact that Julie had so far not been healed is not conclusive evidence of too little faith.

It's also true that faith to be healed is a gift of the Spirit (see Moroni 10:11) and is not necessarily given to everyone (see Moroni 10:17). Those not given this gift are also not condemned in any way. The Lord said, "And again, it shall come to pass that he that hath faith in me to be healed and is not appointed unto death, shall be healed. He who hath faith to see shall see. He who hath faith to hear shall hear. The lame who hath faith to leap shall leap. *And they who have not faith to do these things, but believe in me, have power to become my sons; and inasmuch as they break not my laws thou shalt bear their infirmities*" (D&C 42:48–52; emphasis added). Even if it is true that Julie lacks faith to be healed, that does not mean she is a lesser person in the eyes of the Lord or that her eternal possibilities are therefore limited.

There are many other examples of guilt about nonmoral issues that might be cited. It can be a costly mistake if my attention lapses and I cause a car accident, but this would not necessarily be a moral issue. I might even have inadvertently broken a law and hurt someone in the process, but it's not clearly a moral issue unless I intentionally caused the accident. I might unintentionally say something that hurts someone's feelings, or I might take something from a store without realizing that I hadn't paid for it. As mentioned above, we are responsible for our mistakes, even the innocent ones, and need to make amends where we can. But our behavior is not immoral, and any guilt, beyond the low level variety that might motivate us to apologize and make restitution for our mistake, is unnecessary.

One rule of thumb that might help Latter-day Saints know when guilt is or is not appropriate follows from the temple recommend interview. If we do something that would keep us from a temple recommend, guilt is always appropriate. If our behavior would not keep us from the temple, guilt is likely to be unnecessary. Imagine confessing to the bishop that you haven't been sticking with your diet or that your house is a mess. Rather than deny your recommend, the bishop would probably smile and welcome you to the human race.

Chapter summary

Guilt can indeed be either a blessing or a curse. It's a blessing if it leads to repentance and a curse if it becomes misapplied or extreme. Several guidelines emerge from scripture that can help us avoid unnecessary or unhealthy guilt. These guidelines can be summarized in the following five questions that we can ask ourselves:

1. Do I feel guilty about a sin I have done my best to forsake?
2. Do I feel guilty about something that I cannot directly control?
3. Do I feel guilty about a mistake or shortcoming that's just part of the human condition?
4. Do I feel guilty about a mistake or shortcoming that isn't a moral issue?
5. Is the guilt I feel moving me closer to or further away from Christ?

Related to the subject of guilt, more will be said in a later chapter about the value of repentance and the Atonement in improving and maintaining our emotional and mental health. First, a discussion of perfectionism seems in order. As suggested above, perfectionism is a common source of unnecessary guilt.

Notes
1. David O. McKay, *Gospel Ideals* (Salt Lake City: Improvement Era, 1953), 299.
2. In Conference Report, April 1964, 5.

2 Don't let perfectionism get in the way

AS ELDER RUSSELL M. NELSON has pointed out, "Men are that they might have joy—not guilt trips."[1] Latter-day Saints are a goal-oriented, perfection-bound people. Christ's injunction for us to be perfect (see Matthew 5:48) is an often-remembered indication that individual perfection is both a celestial requirement and a real possibility. Unfortunately, in the pursuit of perfection, some of us end up with too many guilt trips and too little joy. When this happens, it's usually because of one or more of the following *mis*perceptions:

1. Perfection must be achieved in this life.
2. We need to be perfect in everything.
3. Mistakes and perfection are contradicting concepts.
4. We must become perfect entirely by our own effort.
5. To be perfect we must pressure and push ourselves.

Each of these common misperceptions will be discussed below, but first a definition is needed.

What is perfectionism?

Many perfectionists don't realize that the label fits. It's not uncommon to hear them say something like, "Oh, I'm not a perfectionist at all. You should see my house, or my desk at work." Perfectionists are not necessarily perfect in what they do, but they are obsessive in what they think. In fact, it's possible to be so concerned about doing something perfectly that it barely gets done at all. For instance, some people aren't active in the Church because at one time they felt compelled to be the perfect member. Since they weren't perfect (nor is anyone), they became uncomfortable and ended their active involvement. Some perfectionists keep a messy house, not because that's fine in their view, but because their standards are so high that they give up trying. They may pretend not to care, but it's a hollow pretense. Underneath, they are significantly stressed by the lack of order.

It's also true that perfectionism isn't a universal trait. We can be a perfectionist about some things and not others. Some people are obsessive about their weight and physical appearance but not about how clean their home or car is. Others are obsessive about social interactions—making certain they say and do the right things socially—but not about physical appearance. Some are perfectionists when it comes to their family but not about their work. Others are just the opposite.

So, when are we a perfectionist? We are a perfectionist whenever we can't be at peace and feel good about ourselves or others unless something is done, at least close to, perfectly. Wanting to do things perfectly is fine. Striving to do things as perfectly as circumstances will allow is the mark of a successful person. *Needing* to do things perfectly can be a problem. So often in life we don't have the ability to do whatever it is perfectly; or it would take so much time and effort that it's impossible from a practical standpoint. If we can't be comfortable with ourselves or with someone else in those situations, then we are a perfectionist—at least about that particular issue.

In terms of common examples, we are likely a perfectionist if we can't get to sleep unless chores have been done satisfactorily. The label probably fits if we do chores that should be assigned to others because they never seem to do them to our standard. The label might fit if we often redo something that another has done because it wasn't done "right." We are probably a perfectionist if we don't do something nice for someone because we can't be sure what the "right" thing to do is. Perfectionism is a possibility if we are frequently concerned about things that other good people don't seem to care about. We could well be a perfectionist if we qualify for a temple recommend and are striving to be a good person, yet feel guilty and inadequate because of shortcomings in ourselves or our family.

What's wrong with being a perfectionist?

As suggested earlier, perfectionism leads to unnecessary guilt, which is counter motivating and takes us away from important goals—not to mention its negative effect on mental and emotional health. The person who is not active in the Church for reasons of perfectionism, or those who are not comfortable in their faith for that reason, are a case in point. I know a brother who converted to the gospel as an adult. As he attended meetings, he was constantly embarrassed by his lack of knowledge. As questions were posed in the classes he attended, he rarely knew the answers. Rather than accept this as natural for someone just starting out in the Church, he felt like he didn't belong. He kept telling himself that he should know more than he did and that others were so far ahead that he could never catch up. This brother also felt guilty about many other things that are common to many of us—such as not being consistent in his scripture study and the fact that he didn't enjoy going home teaching. Unfortunately for this brother and his family, rather than change his perfectionist expectations and gradually improve himself over time, he quit going to church.

Others continue faithfully but, because of their perfectionism, lose the enjoyment that they would otherwise experience in the gospel. Mission presidents often see missionaries who experience difficulty because they have unrealistic expectations. They become so obsessed or consumed with their every thought, action, and response that they can't enjoy their mission. They often have significant problems getting along with companions, lose the Spirit, and become ineffective teachers. All too often, their perfectionism and the resulting pressures also trigger episodes of depression.

In addition to problems affecting activity in the Church, perfectionism can also lead to a lack of tolerance and charity in family life. Someone who obsessively believes that something must be done perfectly is likely to become manipulative, demanding, and intolerant. Consider the following analogy. I have to breathe in order to stay alive. If someone put a hand over my nose and mouth, they would certainly hear from me. Even though I'm normally mild-mannered, I would kick, bite, maim, or do whatever necessary to breathe. Likewise a parent or spouse thinking that something *must* be done a particular way will do whatever it takes to see that it gets done that way—even to the point of being manipulative, critical, or demeaning. Many strained relationships between spouses, or between parents and children, have this root cause.

A further problem with perfectionism is that it contributes to stress and irritability within the perfectionist. It's humanly impossible to be perfect in all aspects of one's life, which means that those requiring themselves to be perfect will be frequently frustrated. There are also many times in life in which we face contradicting requirements. Perfectionists must complete the project at hand perfectly, but they must also be on time for their next assignment and complete it perfectly as well. Usually it isn't possible to do both, and the perfectionist ends up inevitably disappointed and frustrated for failing on one hand or the other.

A parent can't be perfectly tolerant and also an effective disciplinarian. A person can't be a perfect student and a perfect friend to those who want attention during study time. A golfer can't spend the time required to perfect his game and still be a perfect husband, father, employee, and church member. Something has to give. A "perfect" life requires balance, not extreme performance. Choices have to be made.

But a perfectionist has a hard time making choices. Suppose a perfectionist has a sick friend. The perfect response would be to visit the friend and take food, flowers, or some other remembrance. The perfect response might also include taking care of the sick friend's children for the day or cleaning her house. Since the perfect response is most likely not possible, the perfectionist may end up doing nothing at all. Often perfectionists simply don't have the choice to make a quick telephone call, visit briefly (without a gift), or respond in any way other than in the perfect way. Of course, the perfectionist might also agonize over what the perfect thing to do is in this or any other circumstance. Situations and people vary so much that the perfect thing to do in any given instance usually isn't all that clear. Many give up or wait until the opportunity passes before ever figuring out what the right thing to do is.

Again, there isn't anything wrong with striving to do things perfectly. Doing things to the best of our ability *under the circumstances we face* is most reasonable. Feeling obligated to do things perfectly under any circumstance is not. Interestingly, those who cross the line into perfectionism are often among the most dedicated and committed people among us. They accomplish a great deal but usually fail to recognize or appreciate that fact.

So what do these good people do to overcome this problem? The cure starts with recognizing the common misperceptions that underlie perfectionism, several of which are discussed below.

It's a mistake to think that we must be perfect in this life

Many people quit their celestial pursuit for the same reason that my granddaughter wanted to quit learning to play the piano—practicing is painful. My granddaughter wanted to take a few lessons and wow her friends and family, but of course it doesn't work that way. To her credit (and to her mother's credit for not caving), she has persisted and is turning into an excellent pianist. She still isn't ready for a professional career, but progress is obvious and substantial.

In the same way, none of us will become spiritually perfect with just a few lessons. Apparently we were preparing for eons before this mortal existence, and experience tells us that becoming perfect is a slow process while here. The goal at any given point should be the next level, not the final result. Otherwise we tend to be overcome with a sense of hopelessness. From the bottom of the mountain looking up, it seems as if the goal is impossible. But we can identify the steps necessary to reach the next plateau. Once there, we have a clearer view of the next step, and so on until we reach the summit.

We subvert this necessary step-by-step process if we feel a need to do it all at once. Someone once counted the number of directives issued from the pulpit during a stake conference session—something like thirty-eight by the time the last speaker finished. The directives in total represented a level of performance considerably higher than that of most individuals in the congregation. Rather than let the Spirit direct them regarding where to spend improvement energy most wisely, some considered it their obligation to immediately measure up to all the directives. As a result, they felt that their present steady efforts were not sufficient, they became unhappy with themselves, and they feared that they would never be good enough to be acceptable to the Lord either. This combination of frustration and self-doubt actually led some to lessen their commitment to the gospel. Others made improvements in their life in the short run, but before long they crashed under the weight of unrealistic expectations.

Expecting to immediately follow all of the directives and complete all of the goals suggested by individuals in Church meetings is like going to a banquet and feeling obligated to eat everything there. Information disseminated in Church meetings is almost always good advice, and much of it is essential to exaltation. But we need to pick and choose improvement goals wisely rather than feel obligated to do everything at once. It's not necessary to "run faster than [we have] strength" (Mosiah 4:27). One-step perfection is a concept championed by Lucifer, who knows that it will eventually lead to emotional upset in those who attempt to practice it, as surely as eating too much food leads to stomach upset.

On this same point, in section 67 of the Doctrine and Covenants, the Lord, through Joseph Smith, spoke to early members of the Church about their lack of faith, about their problem with the language of some of the revelations, and about their lack of humility. He concluded, "Ye are not able to abide the presence of God now, neither the ministering of angels; wherefore, continue in patience until ye are perfected. Let not your minds turn back; and when ye are worthy, in mine own due time, ye shall see and know that which was conferred upon you by the hands of my servant Joseph Smith, Jun." (D&C 67:13–14). Generalizing from this message, it appears that, even though we are far from perfect now, the Lord will ultimately bless us if we patiently stay the course and continue to put forth effort to become worthy. It doesn't have to happen today, which is fortunate since it *can't* happen today.

As Elder Russell M. Nelson has said, "We need not be dismayed if our earnest efforts toward perfection now seem so arduous and endless. Perfection is pending. It can come in full only after the Resurrection and only through the Lord. It awaits all who love him and keep his commandments. It includes thrones, kingdoms, principalities, powers, and dominions. It is the end for which we are to endure. It is the eternal perfection that God has in store for each of us."[2]

It's a mistake to think that we must be perfect in everything

We, as Latter-day Saints, get our sense of the need to be perfect from a number of places in scripture. For example, we understand that no unclean thing can enter into God's kingdom (see 3 Nephi 27:19) and that God cannot look on sin with the least degree of allowance (see Alma 45:16). We also understand the fallacy in the common attitude that Nephi predicted would exist in our day, which suggests that God will "justify [us] in committing a little sin" and that we should "lie a little, take the advantage of one because of his words, dig a pit for thy neighbor; there is no harm in this; and do all these things, for tomorrow we die; and if it so be that we are guilty, God will beat us with a few stripes, and at last we shall be saved in the kingdom of God" (2 Nephi 28:8).

On the other hand, we also know from numerous scriptures that we can only be made perfect in Christ (see Moroni 10:32; D&C 76:69). Mistakes and sin are inevitable for us in this life; but the gospel (which means "good news") is that we can be perfected in spite of them—assuming our solid effort to repent and follow the Savior's example. In other words, our sins will not necessarily keep us from being perfected. It's also comforting to know that the Lord will judge us not only according to our works but also according to the desires of our hearts (see D&C 138:9). That gives hope to those of us who put good effort into doing the right things in our lives but still come up short at times.

Our general shortcomings and imperfections that have nothing to do with sin will likewise not keep us from our eternal goal. It goes without saying that no one has the intellect, stamina, time, or talent to do *everything* well, let alone perfectly. Fortunately, we don't have to. Following the Savior's example, we must put effort into loving others, serving them, and keeping God's commandments. But we don't have to be perfect house-keepers or perfect in our job or in our manners. We can forget things, drop the ball on occasion, and muff opportunities. We can lock ourselves out of our car, get lost, and snore loudly—all without eternal consequences.

Interestingly, concerning the Savior's example, we don't know if even Jesus kept his personal belongings in perfect condition, if He always made perfect cuts as a carpenter, or if He had impeccable manners as defined by the times. We do know that none of that was necessary in order to perfectly complete His mission on earth. Although many of us get hung up feeling obligated to do such things perfectly, it just isn't necessary to do so.

Not only is it impossible and unnecessary to do everything perfectly (depending on how we define the term), doing things perfectly can, ironically, sometimes be a mistake. For example, many people think of per-fection as a linear concept. If something is good, then the more of it the better. It's probably more correct to think of perfection as a curvilinear concept. If a thing is good, more of it is better up to a point, but then more may be a problem. Scripture reading is good, but a person theoreti-cally could be so involved in reading scripture that other important things don't get done. Work is necessary and good, but it can certainly be taken to an extreme. A child might think that an unlimited supply of candy would be perfect, but parents know better.

Essentially, rather than extreme performance or an extreme condi-tion in any particular direction, perfection often requires balance. That is clearly true with respect to certain important principles. Mercy, for example, can't be taken to an extreme without robbing justice, nor can justice be taken to extreme without doing violence to mercy (see Alma 12:32; 34:16). Honesty must be tempered with sensitivity and caring. The perfect response socially might be to overlook a fault of another or to downplay it, rather than to be perfectly, and therefore brutally, honest. Perfect discipline is somewhere on a balance point between extremely permissive and extremely restrictive. In fact, with most things, balance is a key element in perfection.

Mistakes and perfection are not contradictory concepts

The only way for a mortal to avoid mistakes is to withdraw from life. Perhaps a hermit sealed off from interaction with others and removed from most of life's responsibilities could exist without making mistakes. But, of course, that kind of lifestyle itself would be a great mistake. We need to be involved with people and to live life fully because experience is a primary objective of mortality. The avenue to celestial perfection involves living, and there is no way to live without making mistakes. In that sense, mistakes and perfection do not contradict one another. Rather, making mistakes and learning from them are necessary parts of the perfection process.

A life without mistakes, or a life of innocence, is apparently the kind of life lived by Adam and Eve prior to the Fall. But their eternal development depended, as ours does now, on living in a world where mistakes are possible. "And now, behold, if Adam had not transgressed he would not have fallen, but he would have remained in the garden of Eden. . . . And they would have had no children; wherefore they would have remained in a state of innocence, having no joy, for they knew no misery; doing no good, for they knew no sin. But behold, all things have been done in the wisdom of him who knoweth all things. Adam fell that men might be; and men are, that they might have joy" (2 Nephi 2:22–25).

Stating the basic concept here in a little different way, several scriptures talk about the value of our weaknesses as part of a growing and learning process (see Ether 12:27–28 and Jacob 4:7). If we are humble, which means having the ability to learn from our mistakes, our weaknesses can lead to strength. It's also comforting to know that the Lord will be patient with us, in spite of our weaknesses, during the learning process. "But now I tell it unto you, and ye are blessed, not because of your iniquity, neither your hearts of unbelief; for verily some of you are guilty before me, but I will be merciful unto your weakness" (D&C 38:14).

Certainly God knows that it isn't in our best interest if we are traumatized by our mistakes. To condemn ourselves or others because of mistakes is like condemning and punishing a child who falls down while learning to walk. How can a child learn to walk without falling down a few times? How can a mortal learn to act perfectly without making mistakes along the way? A child ridiculed or punished for falling down while learning to walk may still learn to walk, but the natural learning process will be disrupted and learning will take longer than usual. The same thing can happen to all of us if we fail to see the value in our mistakes and are overly self-critical. More will be said about this in a later section.

It's a mistake to think we must become perfect solely on the basis of our own effort

As Elder Nelson has pointed out (quoted earlier), we won't become perfect until after the Resurrection, and we will become perfect then *only* through the instrumentality of Jesus Christ. In the closing verses of the Book of Mormon, Moroni invites us to become perfect in Christ (see Moroni 10:32–33). As these verses suggest, after all our struggles with sin, after all our shortcomings and mistakes, God will complete the process for the faithful and bestow upon them His divine nature. Only then will faithful followers of Christ have the power to keep all of the commandments. Only then will they be perfect. This opportunity is the crowning gift of the Savior to those who follow Him. One way of phrasing this truth is to say that we can only become perfect through the grace of Christ. Another way of phrasing the same thing is to say that because of the grace of Christ we can be made perfect even when our best efforts fall short—as they inevitably will. In other words, we don't have to do it alone.

In addition to ultimately carrying us across the goal line, the Lord has promised to help us along the way. Numerous scriptures refer to God's desire to bless us (see 3 Nephi 10:6; Matthew 7:9–11; Matthew 7:7). All we need to do is ask in faith. The Lord has also promised that we will not be tested beyond our ability to cope (see 1 Corinthians 10:13; Alma 13:28; D&C 64:20). Circumstances will be altered and our abilities will be strengthened whenever our own limits are exceeded. This is a comforting promise to those in the middle of disasters that seem overwhelming.

It's a mistake to assume that in order to be perfect we have to put extreme pressure on ourselves

Good emotional and mental health requires that we not be too hard on ourselves. This is a frightening thought for many people who are committed

to a "carrot and stick" motivational philosophy. According to this philosophy, people move forward best if threatened with a stick (criticism), or if
rewards are withheld (acceptance). People who operate by this philosophy
rarely feel good about their accomplishments and are generally self-critical.
They are also typically critical of others, and they have a hard time giving
compliments—at least to people closely related to them. These people tend
to be most critical of those close to them for whom they feel responsible.
That means they are usually most critical of themselves, next their spouse,
then their children, their employees, and on down the line.

Carrot and stick type people are usually committed to their philosophy
in large part because it works. Criticism and withholding of acceptance can
be motivating. Most of us know someone who is extremely successful in
life in large part because they were pushed hard as children. The problem is
that there are usually significant negative side effects involved with pushing
ourselves or others too hard. Too much criticism and too little acceptance
can lower self-esteem, lower self-confidence, and lead to frustration. It can
rob a person of the enjoyment they might otherwise have in their successes
and reduce overall quality of life and happiness. It may also cause people
to give up either on themselves or on their values. They might think, *Why
try to do the right thing if my best effort never seems to be good enough?* Or
perhaps a person might decide that something they are trying to do isn't
the right thing after all since it doesn't seem to make them happy. This
explains why some who were once committed to the Church become less
active or why they give up on their spouse, their parental responsibilities,
efforts to get an advanced education, and so forth.

John is an example of one infected with the carrot and stick philosophy. It started largely with his father, who was extremely difficult to please.
When John mowed the lawn, there was always some complaint, such as
"You missed that spot over there. You didn't sweep up well enough. You
are never going to be successful if you don't pay more attention to details."
John once had all A's and one B on his report card. Pretty much ignoring
the A's, Dad's comment was, "It's obvious you can raise that B grade if
you just put in a little more effort. You know the competition. You aren't
going to get into a great college without straight A's." Dad loved his son
and just wanted the best for him. The problem was he believed that he was
helping John by constantly pushing him to do better and rarely acknowledging John's successes. In fact, his criticism and lack of acceptance were
extremely detrimental.

John, for his part, picked up where his father left off. He became extremely self-critical and unsatisfied with his accomplishments. He grew into being an extremely rigid person and a classic perfectionist—all with unfortunate results. For one thing, John was not successful in college. He simply couldn't decide on a major. It was critical to him that he make the right choice, but he was never sure. He also had extreme test anxiety that interfered with academic performance, and he found himself getting sick a lot and he experienced debilitating periods of depression. His social life suffered because he was either sick, or he was studying all of the time. He also had trouble feeling confident around women; but then he also found that no one he met measured up to his expectations. Since he had tried so hard to live his religion but was still unhappy, he began to doubt his religious roots. This was particularly true since John heard so often from the pulpit and in scripture that "obedience leads to happiness" (see Mosiah 2:41; Alma 41:10). That certainly didn't seem to be true in John's case.

The interesting thing about this last point is that John really had not been living the essence of his religion. He had been doing a great job of living the letter of the law, but he was falling seriously short on charity and tolerance—both for himself and others. Charity, as the Apostle Paul pointed out, is a necessary part of the equation: "Though I speak with the tongues of men and of angels, and have not charity, I am become as sounding brass, or a tinkling cymbal. And though I have the gift of prophecy, and understand all mysteries, and all knowledge; and though I have all faith, so that I could remove mountains, and have not charity, I am nothing. And though I bestow all my goods to feed the poor, and though I give my body to be burned, and have not charity, it profiteth me nothing" (1 Corinthians 13:1–3). John had been trying very hard to live his religion, but it was not paying dividends in his life because he wasn't charitable toward himself and others. He had not been living, to the extent necessary, the law upon which happiness depends (see D&C 130:20).

Charity, or love, is the best motivator in the universe. It is "the pure love of Christ, and it endureth forever, and whoso is found possessed of it at the last day, it shall be well with him" (Moroni 7:47). It's as effective as a carrot and stick approach but without all of the negative side effects. Over time, people will be more likely to keep the commandments if they do so because they love the Lord, they love other people, and they love correct principles. They are then naturally inclined to do good and make good choices because they care, not because they are afraid of what might happen if they don't.

John needed to learn that he can become less self-critical and more accepting of himself (be more charitable) and yet still be motivated to improve himself and be successful. He would then do well in school because he naturally wants to be a success, not because he is afraid of being a failure. He would work to do things as perfectly as possible because it makes sense to do so, not because he is a slothful, unsuccessful person if he doesn't. He would put solid effort into tidying up his life and do even unpleasant chores because he values the good reasons for doing so, not because it is necessary in order to be a successful human being. He would be able to appreciate his accomplishments—which is in itself motivating—and he would escape the problems inherent in living in the negative, critical world that he had created for himself.

As an aside, John's situation is typical in that before he discovered this root cause to many of his emotional problems and became more charitable in his thinking about himself and others, John went to an extreme in the opposite direction. For years he had devoted himself to being the perfect church member. At one point he decided the effort had not only been misplaced, but that it was the cause of most of his problems. Based on that assumption, he went from being an extremely committed member to being extremely anti-LDS. In a similar way, he went from being obsessive about his school work to not doing it at all. John changed the focus of his life in terms of objectives but didn't fix the real problem of his extreme, perfectionist thinking. Happily, he was able eventually to fix this root issue which then gave him the option to be more balanced in his life generally and finally to return to his religion.

In the meantime, John's experience underscored the truth in President Hinckley's observation that "criticism is the forerunner of divorce, the cultivator of rebellion, sometimes a catalyst that leads to failure. In the Church it sows the seed of inactivity and finally apostasy."[3]

Common myths that encourage perfectionism

John, in the preceding example, along with being consistently and regularly criticized by his father, was also taught early a number of maxims that encouraged perfectionism. For example, he heard repeatedly, "If a job is worth doing, it's worth doing well." But if we think about it, many jobs are worth doing whether they are done well or not. For instance, there is value in spending time with a spouse even if the circumstances aren't perfect. There is value in allowing a child to help with a project even if doing so results in a substandard product. Acknowledging a friend in need is worthwhile even if we don't offer the perfect response. There is value in opening the scriptures and reading even if we can't spend more than a few minutes at the time. A light housecleaning is better than no housecleaning at all. In fact, most worthwhile things are worth doing whether they are done well or not. It makes sense to shoot for the best in whatever we do, but when that isn't possible, something is always better than nothing.

John also repeatedly heard as he was growing up, "You need to get your work done before you can play." That maxim was actually true when John was a child, but it became less true the older he got. As a child, John had plenty of discretionary time and he naturally knew how to play. What he needed to learn then was how to work. But as an adult, John knew how to work, but he had forgotten how to play. He was also overwhelmed with much more work than he could ever reasonably do. His studies, for example, were openended—meaning that he could always do more. As an adult, his work, in effect, was never done. Following the maxim he learned in his youth on into adulthood resulted in John having way too little recreation in his life. He missed meeting the essential need we all have to rest sufficiently. Even the Savior put His earthly ministry on hold long enough to spend forty days and forty nights preparing himself for His mission (see JST, Matthew 4:1).

Last, John heard repeatedly the expression, "Do it right the first time or you will just have to do it again." Of course, this is true only if one buys into the notion that whatever one does needs to be done perfectly. As suggested above, this is not necessarily true. A few things, like brain surgery, require doing the job exactly right every time. If I'm undergoing surgery, I hope for a surgeon who believes in doing his job perfectly. However, 99 percent of everything we do isn't that exacting.

Chapter summary

Perfectionism is a significant obstacle to good emotional and mental health. Change is not easy for those affected, but it is possible. Becoming less of a perfectionist begins with agreeing philosophically that it is the right thing to do. As the last two sections indicate, many people are committed to their perfectionism, thinking that it is a requirement if they are to become successful people and reach their eternal goals. Hopefully the preceding discussion is an effective argument against this notion. Based on common misperceptions about the need to become perfect in this life, you might ask yourself the following questions:

1. Do I feel like I have to become perfect in this life?
2. Do I think I have to be perfect in virtually everything I do?
3. Do I believe that I must try to avoid mistakes at all cost?
4. Do I believe that I must become perfect based solely on my own effort?
5. Do I believe that I must put pressure on myself and push myself to be perfect?

If you answered yes to any of these questions, it means that I have so far been unsuccessful in my arguments. You might go back to the relevant section of this chapter and give me another chance. Once perfectionists believe that it is safe to become more accepting and tolerant of themselves, the next step is to work with habits of thought and frames of reference as suggested in the next chapter.

Notes
1. Russell M. Nelson, "Perfection Pending," *Ensign*, Nov. 1995, 86.
2. Ibid.
3. Remarks delivered 18 June 1983 at BYU—Hawaii.

3 Beware of absolute thinking

AS SUGGESTED IN THE PREVIOUS two chapters, those who become mired in guilt or suffer from perfectionism also tend to think in extremes. They often come to absolute, or black and white, conclusions. As can be seen in the examples that follow, this kind of thinking undermines emotional and mental health and interferes with interpersonal relationships. That's no doubt why the Lord in the Sermon on the Mount warned against thinking this way: "And again it is written, thou shalt not forswear thyself, but shalt perform unto the Lord thine oaths; But verily, verily, I say unto you, swear not at all; neither by heaven, for it is God's throne; Nor by the earth, for it is his footstool; Neither shalt thou swear by thy head, because thou canst not make one hair black or white, But let your communication be Yea, yea; Nay, nay; for whatsoever cometh of more than these is evil" (3 Nephi 12:33–37).

When we make covenants with the Lord, such as at baptism and in the temple, it's important that we be absolute in our resolve to keep our promises. One of the last things we want is to be guilty of perjury or lying under oath (forswearing) to God—hence, the first part of the warning cited above. Then the Lord goes on to suggest that in our general thinking and in our relationships with others, it's important that we not be too sure of ourselves. Since we don't have the perfect understanding and knowledge that God does, it's best not to swear to the truth of things, or to be rigid and black and white in our conclusions. Doing so, even if we are right, is off-putting in our relationships with others, and it can lead to unnecessary guilt and perfectionism, with all the associated problems discussed earlier.

Saying this in another way, we certainly need to be committed to the truth and firm in our faith, but we also must balance religious zeal with humility and tolerance in order to avoid becoming rigid and intolerant. A number of verses in scripture talk about serving God with our whole heart, mind, and soul (see D&C 4:2 as an example). Being lukewarm in our faith is not good (see Revelations 3:16), and we need to be valiant in our testimony (see D&C 76:79). For balance, however, any number of scriptures also talk about the need to be humble and tolerant. Art is an example of what can happen when this balance is missing. Art was never known to utter profanity, but he definitely had a "swearing" problem. Contrary to the admonition of the Savior in the Sermon on the Mount, Art took adamant, unyielding positions on many issues.

Some of these were picky, small things. For instance, Art felt strongly that glasses should be placed in cupboards top up in order to avoid the microbes he imagined would be crawling on the drinking surface if they were placed in the cupboard top down. Art swore to his wife that this was a problem and that any right-thinking person would certainly agree. His wife, for her part, believed in placing glasses top down in order to prevent any potential contaminants from falling into the open glass. Art found himself stressed whenever he discovered that his wife had violated his rule, and their relationship suffered when they argued about the issue. The fact is that most people probably never think about this kind of detail, and it doesn't seem to deserve a lot of attention. But it did get Art's attention, and you can imagine what his life was like given that he was equally adamant about a long list of similar things.

On that list, along with inconsequential things like cups in cupboards, were a number of issues that were actually quite important. For example, Art was totally convinced that his children needed more strict discipline. As a result, he was frequently upset when his wife responded in what he considered to be a permissive and ineffective way with their children. On the other hand, his wife strongly disagreed, thinking that their children needed more nurturing and love. A number of very uncomfortable and destructive arguments then ensued in which each parent swore that he or she was right. Rather than taking an unyielding stand, this is clearly a situation in which they should have stuck with "nay, nay" and "yea, yea."

For certain, their absolute commitment to their position was not defensible. If the situation was explained to a group of parenting experts, some would agree with Art, and others would agree with his wife. In fact, both Art and his wife might be "right" in that what works best for Art might not work best for his wife; or what works best for one of their children might not work best for another. Even with the same child, what works best in one situation might not be best in another. There is probably a better and a worse way to proceed in parenting their children, but no absolute rule exists. The best way to discover the ideal response to their children in any given situation lies in both Art and his wife being humble enough to learn from each other and to listen to the Spirit. That won't happen if they swear that they already know the truth.

Interestingly, this need to avoid being absolute in our thinking might even apply to matters of religious philosophy or practice—an area where absolutes are more likely to be found. As an example, "Thou shalt not kill" (Exodus 20:13) sounds like an absolute commandment. But then we have to consider the requirement the Lord placed on Nephi to take Laban's life (1 Nephi 4:10–18). We must also consider the case of soldiers in battle, police officers in the line of duty, and so forth. It appears that there can be exceptions to even apparently absolute rules. As another example, we believe that the temple ceremony was given by God through revelation. Some members, who think like Art, were troubled a few years ago when certain aspects of the ceremony were changed. They tended to think in absolutes about the ceremony and were therefore not prepared to accept the situation when changes were made—also through revelation.

Any number of scriptures tell us that God is the same yesterday, today, and forever (see Hebrews 13:8). His love for us is never failing, as are His objectives, and His eternal law remains the same. There is variability in the details, however, which makes current revelation to the Church, and to each of us personally, so important. It also means that we, as mere mortals, are better off avoiding absolute positions. That way we avoid being stubborn and pigheaded. That way we are in the best position to learn from each other and the Spirit as we grow toward our potential.

"Have to" thinking can be a big problem

One specific example of violating the rule described above occurs when we get into the habit of "have to" thinking. Some people think of virtually everything they do in absolute terms like "have to," "must," or "can't." They say things like, "I 'have to' get out of bed. I 'must' be to work on time, and "I 'can't' be late." As suggested below, habitually thinking this way takes the fun out of things that would otherwise be enjoyable, creates significant stress, and causes irritation and anger. These negative consequences follow in part because people who think that they *must* do something essentially have no choice. Agency—the power and freedom to make choices—is one of those immutable eternal laws. Brigham Young once pointed out that "this is a law which has always existed from all eternity, and will continue to exist throughout the eternities to come. Every intelligent being must have the power of choice."[1] We can't deny this law without negative consequences.

If someone put a gun to my head and demanded that I put forty pounds on my back and hike twenty miles, I would hate every step of the way. If I decided to do the same thing in the context of a backpacking trip, I would likely enjoy it. The difference, of course, lies in my having a choice in the matter. We tend not to enjoy those things that we feel compelled to do. We are not likely to enjoy our religion if we think it is forced on us. Work that we have to do is not that much fun. Even recreational pursuits can be a chore if we think of them in "have to" terms. A golfer thinking that he has to beat his opponent or that he must score better than he did the last time will probably experience more stress than enjoyment from the round—at least assuming he isn't playing his best golf that day.

"Have to" thinking can rob us of the pleasure in otherwise enjoyable things, and it also generates stress. As suggested in the chapter on perfectionism, we can't always do the things that we feel we must do. Sometimes we fall short by reason of our mortal limitations, and sometimes whatever we would like to do is simply beyond our control. Suppose, for example, that I am buying a new car and I think that I *have to* get the best deal possible. First, I may not have the time or energy to put into a comprehensive search, at least not without sacrificing other important things. Second, I don't control many of the variables involved. I don't control profit requirements at various dealerships, dealership inventories, economic variables such as interest rates, particular salesmen or managers on duty at a given dealership, and so forth. I can put great effort into the project and even think I got the best deal possible, only to find that someone else got a similar car for less.

"Have to's" are often contradictory. Suppose a mother decides that she *has to* to spend quality time with a child having a problem. But then the telephone rings, which she *has to* answer. On the phone is a friend with a problem that *has to* be addressed. Given that she can't attend to the needs of both her child and her friend, this mom will inevitably end up stressed.

That stress will be compounded if a number of other requirements exist at the same time. For instance, she may need to get dinner ready, the car she was cleaning is only half done, and the baby has just started to cry. Stress generated by this kind of situation over time is counter-motivating. It can increase susceptibility to health problems, and it generally lowers quality of life.

Frustration at not being able to get things done that need to be done also typically results in irritation and anger. The mom in this case may end up angry with her children—even the one she recognizes has a special need—and she might be irritable with her husband when he gets home. Of course, this mom will also likely be angry at herself. She might think, "I have to get a handle on things. I can't let myself get so angry." Now a new absolute requirement has been added to her life. She not only has to do the impossible, but she has to do it with a good attitude.

Getting away from the "have to's"

Life for all of us includes moments like the one experienced by the mother described above. Most of us have more on our plate than we can reasonably handle. In order not to be overcome with stress, we sometimes need to simplify our life. In some cases it may help to cut back volunteer hours spent each week or to extend deadlines on projects we face. Sometimes it's even necessary to do something major like change careers or sell a home. But most often, the best solution is simply to change how we think about our responsibilities. It's generally not the list of responsibilities, but how we think about them, that determines our stress level. The problem comes from the inevitable frustration experienced if we believe we "have to" do things that are not possible to do. The problem lies in the fact that we sometimes think we have no choice—we have to do it all.

The truth is, there are very few absolute requirements in life. The mother in the example didn't have to attend to the needs of her child. She didn't have to answer the phone or help her friend. She doesn't even have to stay married, continue to care for her children, or go to church. There are obviously good reasons to do all of those things and there are significant negative consequences if she does not, but the choice remains. If she recognizes this choice in how she thinks, she will be able to make choices more comfortably as she picks and chooses between various priorities. She will experience less stress and find more satisfaction in the things that she chooses to do.

For those who have not yet learned to think this way, the process of changing thought habits starts philosophically. We need to realize at a general level that we have all been given our agency and that there is nothing that we are forced to do. Then at a more practical level, we need to apply this understanding to how we think on a day-to-day, moment-to-moment basis. We can begin by listening to how we describe projects and life events. If we hear absolute language, we can change. For instance, even at the very beginning of the day, rather than thinking "I *need* to get out of bed," we can decide to think, "I *want* to get up." Then through the day we can continually be aware of our thinking and make similar changes in how we describe to ourselves the many choices that come up.

This process can be very effective, but those who try it often get confused at first. For one thing, it doesn't naturally feel like we want to do some things. In those cases, it seems like thinking the way suggested is just kidding ourselves. For example, some days, the pull of the mattress is extreme. The last thing we really want to do is leave the comfort of the bed. At the same time, we do want the advantage of getting on with our day. In fact, in the sense of longer-term goals, it's always appropriate to think of even uncomfortable things that we should do as "want to's" rather than "have to's." When we emphasize the benefits of doing the uncomfortable thing in our mind, it's easier to be motivated, and there is an emotional benefit from recognizing our choice in the matter.

As another common problem, it may seem like simply changing how we think in the manner suggested above couldn't possibly make much difference. The impact, however, can be significant. First of all, the effect is cumulative. We think about various tasks hundreds or thousands of times a day. Getting into the habit of thinking each time in terms of "want to" rather than "have to" can make a huge difference. Second, we respond emotionally to what we are thinking at the moment, not to what we might believe in the abstract. Even if we know better at some level, if we think that something *needs* to be done, we will respond emotionally as if it was a legitimate need.

Last, it's common for things to feel like needs even though we are trying to think of them as wants. The negative consequences of some choices are so extreme that even though we technically have a choice, it doesn't feel like it. But there is still benefit in framing those things as a choice, even in those situations. Thinking the words results in reprogramming our thinking and pays an emotional dividend when repeated over time.

A real-life example of the change process

To put this process in the context of a real-life example, consider Jill's experience. Jill was deeply depressed and anxious when I first met her. She felt like a total failure as a human being. She described her situation as being in a very deep hole with no hope of escape. A big part of the reason she felt this way had to do with the fact that, in her mind, she wasn't adequately fulfilling her many responsibilities. Indeed, Jill had a long list of duties relative to her five children, her husband, home, neighbors, friends, and church. Some things on her list were more important than others. Some were pleasurable, like reading with her children or going skiing with her family. Others, such as doing laundry and cleaning bathrooms, were not so pleasant. She also had items on her list of things to do that were potentially relaxing, such as pleasure reading and visits with friends.

In short, this was a list like most of us have. It was long and complex, but relatively ordinary. Of course, the problem wasn't the list itself, but how Jill thought about her responsibilities. Everything on her list was a "have to." She didn't see any choice about fixing dinner for her family every night or keeping her house clean. She saw no choice about enrolling her children in soccer and other activities. She had to meet all neighborhood and church responsibilities as they came up, or she felt like a failure. Even the pleasurable activities on her list were thought of as obligations.

Since virtually everything on her list was a "have to," it was naturally very difficult to make decisions about how to spend her time. How does one prioritize when, in effect, everything carries the same high priority? Of course, Jill realized that some things on her list were more important than others, but her frame of reference basically nullified the benefit of that understanding. She operated emotionally, as if everything was of equal priority. This made it difficult, if not impossible, when she was sick or otherwise not able to do the things that she "needed" to do. She couldn't hire help, modify plans, or ask for favors without feeling guilty.

Regarding her personal time, Jill frequently ended up in a lose/lose situation. If she decided to do something fun for herself, she felt guilty and couldn't really enjoy the activity because of all the other things that she had to do. If she stayed home to clean the house or meet some other obligation, she resented having to stay home. Her husband, on the other hand, seemed to be able to drop obligations and go off and do something fun at a moment's notice. It was Jill that always ended up the responsible one doing the hard things while everyone else was able to do whatever they wanted. As a result, Jill was frequently frustrated and angry at her husband and children. Then she would get angry with herself for being angry with them.

All of this created a sense of failure that wore Jill down over time, reducing her self-esteem, her confidence, and her enjoyment of life. The related problems she had in her marriage and other personal relationships pushed her further into a cycle of anxiety and depression. That's all the bad news. The good news is that she was able to surface from the deep hole she made for herself simply by changing her thinking.

At least the concept was simple. The actual process of change took considerable time and effort. The strategy she employed had four main elements. First, Jill had to listen to her thinking and consciously make changes along the lines suggested above. Further, this effort had to be continued over several weeks before it began to pay dividends in her emotional life. Second, Jill had to learn to say no to some requests. Doing so proved to be painful until she learned to control her thinking in ways that reduced the unnecessary guilt. Third, Jill had to confront some of her perfectionist thinking such as learning that it's okay to play before all of her work is done. She had to learn that some things are worth doing even if they aren't done well and that it's okay if some important things don't get done at all. Fourth, Jill restructured her environment in several ways. For instance, she had been doing more for her children than was healthy for her to do. Changes needed to be made in chore assignments and other expectations of her children. She also ended up working around her husband's peculiarities in a new way.

Jill's husband had subconsciously learned to take advantage of his wife. He knew that if he procrastinated long enough Jill's "have to's" would take over and she would do whatever needed to be done. It's therefore not surprising that he was a world-class procrastinator at home. Jill's husband furthermore didn't care about some things that were quite important to Jill. As an example, he didn't much care about keeping his car clean. Jill, on the other hand, was deeply embarrassed if his car was dirty. For years, she had therefore assumed responsibility to wash her husband's car and clean it out on a regular basis.

Jill decided that she would no longer care about her husband's dirty car and similar issues that were really his responsibility anyway. If her husband kept his car dirty, that was his problem. She would use it as little as possible, and when it was necessary to drive it, she kept reminding herself that she could keep her car any way she chose, but the condition of her husband's car just didn't matter to her. In other instances where her husband's procrastination affected Jill in ways that were hard to ignore, Jill became assertive. To deal with her husband's junk in the garage, which had been piling up for years, Jill gave him an ultimatum. She gave him a reasonable time to clean up the garage after which time she would get some help and clean it out herself. Not surprisingly, her husband didn't get around to the task, and Jill ended up following through with her threat. This caused some friction in their marriage, but the conflict experienced was significantly less serious than the problems caused by Jill's ongoing emotionalism and obsessive behavior prior to the changes she made.

As Jill became less absolute in her thinking, her relationship with her husband and children improved. Her emotional and mental health were also greatly enhanced. She even experienced a quite unexpected benefit. By being less concerned about getting everything on her list done, she was actually more productive. As she thought about everything in terms of "want to" rather than "have to," she found that she was more creative in solving scheduling problems, combining activities, and doing other things that improved her productivity. She also experienced a higher energy level and was sick far less often. All in all, she found that the effort required to change her habit of absolute thinking to be very much worthwhile.

Avoid thinking in terms of "never" and "always"

Another example of thinking in absolutes—swearing as the Lord warned against in the Sermon on the Mount—involves describing events or circumstances in terms of "never" or "always." Thinking this way leads to errors in judgement and encourages jumping to conclusions as described in the next section. It can also lead to a premature sense of failure or a loss of motivation when working on self-improvement goals.

Suppose, for example, that I am trying to overcome some bad habit, and I make a vow to myself (swear) that "I will never do that again" or "I will always . . ." This kind of thinking places me in a pass/fail situation in which just one more mistake is fatal. That's a frightening position to be in and leads to hopelessness if I make that additional mistake. It's more realistic, and actually more motivating, to allow room for partial credit, second chances, and learning from mistakes. This frame of reference seems to better fit the vision created by the gospel plan of happiness.

It seems clear in scripture that it's not over until it's over (see for example the parable of the laborers in Matthew 20:1–16). Persistence and continuing the effort are more important than immediate success.

Thinking in terms of "never" and "always" can also lead to extreme self-judgments—usually, but not necessarily, negative ones. If I make a mistake, I might think I'm a total idiot. If I'm late to work one morning, I'm lazy and good-for-nothing. If I lose my cool with one of my children, I'm out of control. This kind of thinking, when taken seriously and repeated over time, takes a significant toll on self-esteem and self-confidence. The truth is that mistakes, shortcomings, and failures don't define us. Our values and the attempts we make to learn from our mistakes are what count. And even values and effort don't necessarily define us—at least beyond the moment. We can change our values and become motivated in ways that we never were before.

Along with negative conclusions about ourselves, we can also err by thinking in absolutes in a positive direction. If something goes well, we might think that everything is right with us and the world and ignore some important problem that needs to be addressed. If we conquer a bad habit, we might think that we never need worry about that problem again, and thus become over-confident. If things are going well in our life, we might jump to the conclusion that we are capable of handling life on our own without help. We might, as the scriptures say, end up trusting in the arm of flesh (2 Nephi 4:34). Thinking in absolutes can lead us into this trap.

Other problems with jumping to extreme conclusions

The preceding discussion refers to the problems that arise when we make absolute judgments about ourselves. We also get into big trouble when we leap from limited evidence to general conclusions. We make this mistake when we decide that because one aspect of a relationship is flawed, the whole relationship has a problem. As a matter of fact, we make that mistake when we decide that one aspect of anything defines the whole. Following are several common examples:

1. He doesn't like _____ about me, so he must not like me at all.

When someone we care about is unhappy with some aspect of our personality, body, or behavior, we sometimes jump to the conclusion that we are unloved or unappreciated in general. As an example, suppose a wife suspects that her husband is unhappy about her weight. He might even (foolishly) admit it. She might then assume that he couldn't possibly be attracted to her, and she might even go as far as to believe that he no longer loves her. The truth is that her husband can love her very much and remain attracted to her even if he has a problem with her weight. The fact of having a problem in one respect does not mean that a problem exists in all respects. As another example, a husband might come to the conclusion that his wife doesn't love and value him because she isn't as interested as he would like her to be in making love. Libido waxes and wanes in any given person over time and varies between people for a myriad of reasons. Problems in this area are important and need to be addressed, but they are not *prima facie* evidence that a partner is unloved.

Along these same lines, it's also true that general satisfaction with a relationship tends to change with time. If your spouse is obviously not feeling very loving toward you on any given day, it doesn't mean that he or she has fallen out of love or will never again feel close. In general, my wife and I deeply love one another and value our relationship. In spite of this, there are times when we don't appreciate each other and wonder why we ever got married in the first place. It would be easy during the down times for one or the other of us to jump to the conclusion that we are generally unloved. But that would be far from the truth. First, there are many more good days than bad. Second, there is an underlying love and commitment that sees us through the times in which we disappoint each other.

Jumping to absolute conclusions, as in the examples given above, creates unhealthy emotion. It also can become a self-fulling prophecy. For instance, partners feeling unloved may deny or ignore evidence to the contrary and continually exaggerate the negatives. In the process of doing so they may become needy and demanding, which actually makes them a less appealing spouse and significantly disturbs their relationship. One of the quickest ways to upset a relationship is to be argumentative or overly analytical about what's going on with it and then to demand that it improve.

2. "I've gained ten pounds. My eating is totally out of control."

Gaining ten pounds is an indication that a person either needs to eat a little less or exercise a little more, but it doesn't necessarily mean that their eating is "totally out of control." One young lady I worked with had gained a few pounds and described herself as totally fat and her eating as totally out of control. As a result she decided to drastically change her diet and spend an hour or so a day exercising. It was very difficult for her to get motivated to make these dramatic changes in her behavior and, as a result, her efforts were sporadic and short-lived. She soon lost faith in her ability to control herself and essentially gave up trying. Ironically, this led to excessive and unhealthy eating.

The fact is that this young lady wasn't that overweight to start with, and she didn't need to make drastic changes in her lifestyle. In her case, all she needed to do was cut back on the several Coca-Colas that she habitually consumed each day. The calories she saved from that alone (empty calories even) would have corrected the weight gain problem. Sadly, by going beyond the mark, she had actually ended up with the problem she originally only assumed.

As in this young lady's case, people who exaggerate their problems tend to come up with exaggerated solutions. Not surprisingly, they then find it difficult or impossible to reach the unrealistic goals they establish. This leaves them frustrated and struggling with self-doubt. A more realistic definition of our problems—avoiding extreme descriptions—results in more realistic goals and a much better chance of success.

3. "She didn't appreciate my gift. Nothing I do for her is appreciated."

Sandra went out of her way to recognize a friend's birthday. She spent considerable time finding a card that said exactly what she wanted to say, and she bought a relatively expensive gift. Her friend didn't call at all for several days, and then when she did, the thanks expressed was routine and not the enthusiastic response that Sandra expected. Based on the lukewarm expression of gratitude, Sandra came to several rather extreme assumptions. She first concluded that her friend didn't appreciate the gift. "Obviously, it wasn't that big a deal to her," Sandra decided. She further assumed that her friend was unappreciative in general. "Nothing I ever do is appreciated. That's the last time I'm going to do something nice for her." Sandra also went the next step and assumed that her efforts to please others in general never seemed to work. "Nothing I ever do for anyone is appreciated. Why bother?"

These were all extreme and misguided conclusions. In fact, Sandra's friend appreciated the gift very much. She intended to call Sandra at the time but got distracted with family and work issues. The friend was still in a crisis mode and somewhat distracted when she finally did get around to calling, which explains the less than enthusiastic response. Furthermore, Sandra's friend was not naturally as effusive as some are. Her responses were often muted compared to others. For these reasons it was a mistake to conclude that Sandra's gift was not appreciated by this friend. And it was an even bigger error to assume that *nothing* she ever did for this friend, or anyone else for that matter, was ever appreciated. Sandra's memory was affected by focusing on the immediate example. If she thought about it honestly, there were many instances in her life in which people made it obvious that they appreciated Sandra's gifts.

Of course, in addition to coming to extreme conclusions about her friend's response to her efforts, Sandra can be faulted for giving gifts with strings attached in the first place. Elder Maxwell expressed on one occasion, "Alas, even when you and I do place something on the altar, we sometimes hang around as if waiting for a receipt."[2] The ideal is always to do nice things for people just because we want to do something nice (see Matthew 6:3), not to feel appreciated or to ingratiate ourselves with others in some way. But Sandra's habit of thinking in extremes made living this principle difficult. Constantly thinking in extremes lowered her self-confidence, which, in turn, resulted in an exaggerated need to get attention and appreciation from others.

There are a number of other common examples of jumping to extreme conclusions on the basis of limited evidence. Some examples include: "My boss never says anything positive about my work." "He lied to me. I can never trust him again." "I thought she liked to visit my family, but obviously she doesn't." "I thought he liked peanut butter sandwiches, but he apparently hates them." Such conclusions are always suspect. Your boss may rarely give positive feedback, but it's not likely that he never does. It's always upsetting and undermines trust when someone close to us lies about something. But people make mistakes. Those we care about can repent and improve themselves, and we can forgive and move on when offended. Moods and preferences are transient. If your partner has a problem one day with your relatives, peanut butter sandwiches, or anything else, it doesn't mean that you were deceived when you earlier thought that the reaction was positive. Likewise, it doesn't mean that whatever problem or preference exists in the present must necessarily persist over time.

Thinking in extremes often causes extreme emotion. It further leads to misjudging ourselves and others in ways that upset interpersonal relationships. We may assume rejection or threat when neither is warranted. We may decide we have been deceived when that's not the case. Or we may decide that we have a problem in a relationship when no problem exists—at least not until we react on our assumption in ways that cause problems. In short, there are a number of reasons to follow the Lord's advice to be moderate in our thinking.

Chapter summary

Potentially frustrating issues we face in life require flexibility, or the "yea, yea" and "nay, nay" spoken of in scripture. While being firm in our faith and committed to our important goals, it's important that we avoid swearing to the truth of things. Saying this in another way, we can uphold our values without being inflexible, unyielding, and inclined to take black and white stands on issues. You might ask yourself the following questions as an indication of whether or not you have a problem in this area:

1. Do I habitually describe projects and tasks in terms of "have to" rather than "want to"?
2. Do I get extraordinarily upset when things don't happen that should happen, or when things do happen that should not?
3. Do I habitually use the terms "never" and "always" in describing events and circumstances in my behavior or in the behavior of others?
4. Do I jump to general conclusions on the basis of one, or just a few, instances of something?

As we avoid thinking in absolutes, we will enjoy better mental and emotional health, as well as improved relationships with others. It will also make it easier for us to have a positive outlook, which is the subject of the next chapter.

Notes
1. Brigham Young, *Discourses of Brigham Young*, compiled by John A. Widtsoe (Salt Lake City: Deseret Book, 1954), 62.
2. Neal A. Maxwell, "Apply the Atoning Blood of Christ," *Ensign*, Nov. 1997, 22.

4 Let in the light

THE SAVIOR TAUGHT THAT "the light of the body is the eye; if, therefore, thine eye be single, thy whole body shall be full of light. But if thine eye be evil, thy whole body shall be full of darkness. If, therefore, the light that is in thee be darkness, how great is that darkness" (3 Nephi 13:22–23). Among other interpretations, the Lord might be pointing to the fact that what we think (see), or at least the focus of our thoughts, largely determines our feelings and the choices we make. If we tend to see mostly the negative, our whole soul will be filled with darkness. We will then suffer emotionally and be more inclined to make poor decisions in life. If we focus on the positive, our whole soul will be filled with light. We will then be happier and make more productive choices.

Stephanie is an example of someone with a habit of dwelling on the negative. For whatever reason, Stephanie developed this habit when she was young. Rather than enjoy the several friends she had, she thought mostly about the one or two classmates that didn't seem to like her. Rather than be happy about the nine questions out of ten that she answered correctly on a quiz, she would be overly concerned about the question she missed. Instead of appreciating the many positive things about her physical appearance, she became distraught over a blemish or some slightly less than perfect feature. It seemed that no matter what the subject, her focus would fix on what was wrong rather than what was right.

Even early in her life, this habit had the consequence predicted by the Lord. In spite of enjoying a basically positive environment, Stephanie was a relatively unhappy child. She was often moody and socially withdrawn.

Of course, her negativism contributed to social problems. No one enjoys the companionship of a withdrawn, pessimistic, and negative person. Stephanie also found it hard to commit to positive goals. She wouldn't try out for sports, join clubs, try to make new friends, or extend herself beyond her limited comfort zone.

As she grew older, the implications of her negative thinking compounded. She eventually married, but to an abusive alcoholic. That poor decision was made largely because of her low self-esteem fueled by the habit of always dwelling on negatives about herself. She became involved with drugs in order to escape, at least temporarily, from the uncomfortable world she had created by her negative outlook. She also found it difficult to commit to positive goals like education, career enhancement, or even hobbies and recreational opportunities. She lacked faith that she could ever be successful, and things seldom worked out, so why bother? In essence, by seeing mostly the negatives in her life, her whole soul became dark, and as a result she made decisions that dramatically multiplied the problems she faced.

The truth is that Stephanie had a choice in how she thought about herself and the events in her life. It was a habit, not a requirement, that she dwell primarily on the negatives. Granted it was a well ingrained habit, one she had had since childhood, but it was still just a habit. And as with any habit, it was amenable to change. It was possible for Stephanie to see the good in even the negative aspects of her life.

Following is a partial list of some of the more significant negative factors in Stephanie's life at the time I met her:

1. She had made a big mistake in deciding to marry the person she did.
2. She stayed in the abusive relationship too long, resulting in problems for both Stephanie and her daughter.
3. Because of the need to work full-time, Stephanie was not spending enough time with her daughter.
4. Stephanie didn't have a lot of friends or social opportunities.
5. On account of their manipulations and constant criticism of whatever she did, Stephanie had largely cut off interactions with her extended family.
6. Stephanie smoked cigarettes and occasionally used marijuana.
7. Stephanie wanted to attend church but didn't, nor did she take her daughter.

Stephanie's habit was to emphasize these and other negatives and to soundly criticize herself because of them. She saw herself as a total failure in each of these problems. There were, however, positive aspects to even these negative issues in her life.

1. Stephanie recognized her mistake and took the necessary steps to protect herself and her daughter from abuse in her former marriage.
2. It took great courage and resolve to break away, and stay away, from her former husband.
3. Stephanie spent all the time she had available with her daughter. Some things fell through the cracks, but they did projects together, read together, and played together.
4. Stephanie had friends, but she didn't have a lot of time to spend with them. She did the best she could, given the priorities in her life of work and her daughter.
5. As hard as it was, Stephanie set boundaries to protect herself from negative interactions with her extended family.
6. Stephanie had overcome the habit of using marijuana daily and used it rarely. She never smoked cigarettes in the car with her daughter or in their apartment.
7. Stephanie made it a point to teach moral lessons to her daughter at every opportunity. They frequently read Bible stories together, and they said a family prayer every night.

Some might think that if Stephanie focuses on the positives in her life and doesn't dwell on the negatives, she is just deceiving herself. It may sound like nothing more than spin control—distorting the truth as many political or lawyerly "spin masters" do in order to make something that is patently unacceptable seem acceptable. The fact is, however, that items on the second list above are equally as true as items on the first list. The negatives in her life need to be dealt with, and more will be said about that later, but Stephanie would not be distorting the truth to focus on the positive aspects of her situation.

Sadly, as indicated above, this didn't happen naturally or easily. Stephanie was obsessed with the negatives on the first list. These thoughts, and many other negative concerns, consumed her thinking with devastating emotional consequences. As a matter of fact, until it was pointed out, she had never even thought about the positives on the second list. The negative filter through which she viewed herself and the world made everything dark. It took some effort for her to even glimpse, let alone really see, the positives in her life.

In order to let the light in, Stephanie had to break her long standing habit of focusing on the negatives. She needed to follow the admonition of Paul as indicated in the last part of the thirteenth article of faith: "If there is anything virtuous, lovely, or of good report or praiseworthy, we seek after these things."

Rather than focusing on the several problems with her job, she could ask herself, "What's good about it?" Her job was stressful and she had a difficult supervisor, but the pay and benefits were excellent, and she enjoyed several of her coworkers. Certain days at work were terrible, but many were quite enjoyable. She could ask the same questions about her extended family. They were generally difficult to relate to, and the boundaries she had established to protect herself from their criticism were appropriate. But when she looked for the good, even in them, she was able to find it. Some of her relatives were actually reasonable, and she enjoyed being with them. Even the most critical had some redeeming qualities Stephanie could see when she looked long and hard enough.

With respect to work, family, and all other issues, Stephanie went on a campaign to discover all that was virtuous, lovely, praiseworthy, and of good report. This was not easy given her longstanding habit of dwelling on negatives, but associating with positive people helped. Visits with her bishop were valuable in this regard, and counseling was helpful. She had good friends who, at her request, helped her look for the positive and gently reminded her when she had fallen back into old habits.

It was also helpful to enlist her daughter in the project. Actually, her daughter had begun to develop a similar habit, and it was most helpful to both mother and daughter as they worked together to see the positive in themselves and the world. They even made a game out of it. Stephanie made some smiley faces and placed them around their apartment as a reminder. She also made a chart to which upside down smiley faces could be attached when it was obvious that either mother or daughter was stuck on a negative perspective. It was fun to watch the number of frowning faces go down over time.

Stephanie found that by focusing on the positives, she didn't just ignore the negatives. Problems in her life continued to be obvious. But with her new outlook, Stephanie was happier, healthier, and better able to address her problems. She was more successful in her self-improvement goals and better able to accept negative situations that she could do nothing about. As dark as her soul had been, she found herself filled with light as she persisted in perceiving herself and her world through a more positive frame of reference.

Stephanie also found the truth in another implication of the Savior's comment that "no man can serve two masters; for either he will hate the one and love the other, or else he will hold to the one and despise the other. Ye cannot serve God and Mammon" (3 Nephi 13:24). In the Book of Mormon, this statement comes immediately after the words of the Lord, quoted earlier, about the light of the body being the eye. Stephanie couldn't be both a positive and a negative person at the same time. Darkness and light don't exist together since one replaces the other. When she focused on the negative, there was no room for light. When she focused on the positive, there was no room in her soul for darkness. Therefore, all Stephanie had to do was work on becoming more positive in her outlook, and the problem with negativity took care of itself.

Look at the donut and not the hole

Putting Stephanie's experience in the context of a metaphor, Stephanie had a long standing habit of looking too much at the hole and not the donut. There is both positive and negative in everything we experience in this life (2 Nephi 2:11–16). What we feel about something is controlled by whether we focus on the positive or the negative piece—the donut or the hole. Among other things, this can seriously affect our close relationships.

Jared and Ann White have a difficult marriage. Jared White, like all of us, is still evolving into what he will eventually become. Following is a partial list of his positive and negative characteristics at the moment.

Positives	Negatives
Works hard on his job	Watches too much TV
Goes to church regularly	Rarely does home teaching
Helps at home when asked	Not a self-starter
Honors his marriage covenant	Not at all romantic
Loves his children	Ineffective disciplinarian
Controls his temper	Doesn't share feelings

Unfortunately, Jared's wife consistently focuses on her husband's negative characteristics and largely dismisses the positive. This judgmental attitude diminishes the love and respect she once had for Jared and leaves her feeling unfulfilled in her marriage. Feeling unfulfilled has contributed to a roving eye as she compares her husband to others, and it has left Ann vulnerable to infidelity. Naturally, her nagging and intolerant attitude has also been upsetting to Jared. He has lost confidence in himself and the resentment he feels toward his wife has reduced his motivation to improve his personality and marriage.

As is all too common, Ann blames Jared for the fact that she is so unhappy in their marriage, and Jared blames Ann. Looking at Ann's part of the problem, a typical conversation she has with herself (as well as with others on occasion) includes thoughts like: "He is totally unromantic, and I can't talk to him about anything." "It upsets me that he doesn't follow through on his church assignments, and he doesn't lead in the home." "He's a wimp with the kids. We are going to have huge problems if he continues to coddle them." "I do everything around the house, and he just sits on his duff and lets me do it."

With this kind of thinking, it's not surprising that Ann feels the way she does. What Ann doesn't see is that she has a choice in how she thinks. There is a long list of positives about Jared that she could focus on if she chose to. It has become her habit, *but she is not compelled*, to focus only on the negative.

Once Ann makes the choice about where to place her focus, she is locked into a particular feeling. If she dwells on the negative, it won't be possible to have loving feelings for her husband or to respect him. If she dwells on the positive, loving feelings and respect will come naturally. Obviously, Jared has a number of shortcomings, and the problems in the marriage are not all Ann's fault. At the same time, Ann must understand that her tendency to focus on the negative is a large part of the problem. That tendency alone is enough to ruin her marriage no matter what problems her husband has.

Actually, Ann knows all of this at some level, but she is afraid to be positive about her husband. She is operating on the misguided belief that overlooking Jared's weaknesses would send the message that she condones his imperfections. She actually believes that by pointing out his flaws she can motivate him to improve. The truth is exactly the opposite. Ann desperately needs to follow the advice of scripture and be less judgmental and more forgiving as discussed in more detail in the next chapter.

The point here is that when we choose to dwell on the hole rather than the donut, we can ruin most anything in our life. Our marriage will start to look like a mistake, we will hate our job, and our home and everything else will disappoint us. As an example, earlier in my life I recall comfortably driving my car to work until a good friend bought a beautiful new model. When he took me for a ride, I was enveloped in the new car smell, and I became jealous of the bells and whistles that his car had that mine didn't. On my next commute, it was amazing how many problems I noticed in my car. Scratches and dents jumped out. Missing features were painfully obvious, and the whole experience was negative. Obviously nothing had changed in my car from one ride to the next, but there had been a big change in my perception. This change in my thinking ruined my car for me until I got back to thinking about its positives rather than its negatives. It wasn't as pretty as the new model, but the fact that it was dependable and paid for made it once again fine with me.

Don't be too analytical

The tendency some have to be overly analytical contributes to a habit of focusing on what's wrong rather than what's right in the world. The fact is that virtually anything that is looked at closely enough will have flaws. If those flaws are then emphasized, anything will appear to be without merit, even when what is rejected is of inestimable worth. For instance, President Hinckley has pointed out how the tendency to focus on negatives stands in the way of some people accepting the truth about the restored gospel. He said:

> We have critics who appear to cull out of a vast panorama of information those items which demean and belittle some men and women of the past who worked so hard in laying the foundation of this great cause. They find readers of their works who seem to delight in picking up these tidbits, in chewing them over and relishing them. In so doing they are savoring some small morsel, rather than eating a beautiful and satisfying dinner of many courses. . . . To highlight mistakes and gloss over the greater good is to draw a caricature. Caricatures are amusing, but they are often ugly and dishonest. A man may have a wart on his cheek and still have a face of beauty and strength, but if the wart is emphasized unduly in relation to his other features, the portrait is lacking in integrity.[1]

This happens whenever we fixate on the flaw in ourselves or another and fail to see the infinite value there. A classic example of this in scripture is found in the eighth chapter of John in the New Testament. A woman was caught in the act of adultery, and her accusers asked Jesus if she should be stoned, as required by the Mosaic law. The Savior's response, you will remember, was, "He that is without sin among you, let him first cast a stone at her" (John 8:7). After the woman's accusers drifted away, convicted by their own consciences, Jesus said to the woman, "Woman, where are those thine accusers? hath no man condemned thee?" When she responded, "No man, Lord," Jesus replied, "Neither do I condemn thee; go, and sin no more" (see John 8:3–11).

This woman's accusers were focusing on the bad and not the good in this woman. The Lord, on the other hand, did just the opposite. But in focusing on the good, the Lord did not ignore the evil. She was required to "go and sin no more." The Lord clearly condemns adultery, even to the point of condemning an adulterous thought (see 3 Nephi 12:27–32), but He didn't condemn this woman. In effect, the sin was condemned here, but not the sinner. To do otherwise would have distorted the truth about this lady. The truth is that, in spite of her sin, she was a child of God with infinite potential. Obviously, if she persisted in her current behavior she would be damned (stopped in her eternal progression). But her sin did not define her. As a matter of fact, her behavior stood in stark contrast to the real truth about this woman. The Savior certainly understood that if she focused on the truth about herself, she would have more motivation and strength to repent and overcome her weakness. This could only happen if she let the light in by dwelling on the positive and not the negative.

Isolating negatives and failing to see them in the context of a larger positive whole can rob us of light in our soul. The same thing is true for those who ask too many "why" questions—or at least, those who ask too many of the wrong kind of "why" questions. Some of the most important questions we can ask in this life are "Why does the world exist?" and "Why am I here?" Testimonies are gained and strengthened as individuals seek answers to these kinds of questions through scripture and prayer. Wondering why things operate as they do is likewise appropriate as a catalyst for learning. On the other hand, some kinds of "why" questions are best left unasked. "Why did this happen to me?" "Why did I do that?" "Why can't I seem to get my life on track?" "Why did he do that?" "Why can't he learn?" Questions like these are rarely productive and almost inevitably lead us to focus on the negative.

Eric is an example of someone troubled by this bad habit. When adversity strikes, Eric is inclined to ask, "Why me?" Unfortunately there is never a clear answer to this question, and Eric's usual attempts to define the answer tend to revolve around negatives: "Because I've disappointed God in some way." "Because I'm unlucky." "Because nothing ever works out for me." The fact of simply asking the question results in negative conclusions or a destructive rehash of all the things wrong about himself and his life. The same thing happens when Eric asks why other people do whatever they do that offends him. "Why did he do that?" Again, the potential answers he comes up with are usually negative: "Because he doesn't like me." "Because he's a jerk." "Because I must deserve it for some reason."

Eric also habitually asks a lot of "why" questions based on assumptions that something is wrong, when, in fact, there may be no problem at all. For example, Eric was engaged to a wonderful woman who clearly met all of his requirements for a future wife. Eric was in love with her but had persistent doubts that came up periodically. These doubts had led him to call off the engagement once already, and his doubts were causing a problem again as the wedding date approached. Eric's worries centered in a perfectionist attitude (see chapter 3) but were definitely fed by asking too many "why" questions. For example, he generally enjoyed his fianceé's company and looked forward to spending time with her. There were other times when he wanted to be alone, or when calling to check in with her seemed more like a duty than a pleasure. At those times, he kept asking, "Why do I feel this way?" The implication, of course, was that there was something wrong with his feelings, and the answers to the question that naturally came to his mind fueled his worries. "I must not really love her after all." "Maybe the Lord is trying to warn me not to marry this lady."

The fact is that the kinds of feelings he had are normal. In the best of relationships, partners may prefer to be alone at times or with someone else. Checking in is a joy at times but may feel like a burden at others. It's also common, in general, to have second thoughts and doubts when facing an important decision like marriage. Such misgivings were not evidence that Eric was about to make a bad decision. But by failing to accept these feelings as normal, and in asking "why" too often, Eric reinforced the very concerns that he was worried about in the first place.

Since some questions in this life don't have answers, and since we often can't see beyond a limited mortal perspective, it's important to do the best we can to make good choices and then move forward with faith. Elder Maxwell put it this way: "What is needed is mortal submission, even when there is no immediate divine explanation. Thus we are to press forward, whatever the length of the near horizon, while rejoicing in what awaits us on the far horizon."[2] More will be said about the power of faith as it relates to our emotional and mental health in a later chapter.

Unhealthy optimism

Following the principles taught in scripture, and as underscored by the examples given so far in this chapter, we all need to develop a positive focus in life. On the other hand, as mentioned in the previous chapter, all good things can be taken to an extreme. It is possible to be too optimistic. Eric, in the preceding example, overanalyzed his decision, but being overly confident of success and moving forward without care would have been a mistake in the opposite direction. It would likewise be dangerous if Eric was so optimistic about future earnings that he overspent or failed to save for potential emergencies. He could have a big problem if he felt optimistically invulnerable and neglected his health or engaged in other risky behavior.

In a similar vein, it sometimes helps to take a pessimistic view. For example, a job candidate may assume that an interviewer will ask hard questions and prepare answers for what might come up in the interview. A person can assume bad weather and have plan B ready just in case. Someone might anticipate a traffic problem and take public transit or leave early. Planning ahead and being prepared for problems can reduce anxiety when facing difficult situations, and it can help smooth the way when difficulties with plans arise. An optimistic attitude has become extreme when it substitutes for actual planning and preparation.

Optimism is likewise overdone if it leads one to be complacent about the consequences of his sins. Nephi clearly described this problem as it would exist in our day: "And there shall also be many which shall say: Eat, drink, and be merry; nevertheless, fear God—he will justify in committing a little sin; yea, lie a little, take the advantage of one because of his words, dig a pit for thy neighbor; there is no harm in this; and do all these things, for tomorrow we die; and if it so be that we are guilty, God will beat us with a few stripes, and at the last we shall be saved in the kingdom of God" (2 Nephi 28:8). Nephi goes on to describe this kind of thinking as "false and vain and foolish doctrines" (v. 9).

Naturally, one big problem that makes the philosophy "eat, drink, and be merry for tomorrow we die" so foolish is that we don't die tomorrow. We go on living and experiencing the consequences of our choices. For this reason, a good part of scripture sounds a negative tone. In the preface to the Doctrine and Covenants, the Lord said, "The voice of warning shall be unto all people, by the mouths of my disciples, whom I have chosen in these last days" (D&C 1:4). And in another place, "For this is a day of warning, and not a day of many words" (D&C 63:58). Christ in teaching his Apostles said, "Think not that I am come to send peace on earth: I came not to send peace, but a sword" (Matthew 10:34).

None of this contradicts the requirement to let in the light by maintaining a positive frame of reference in this life. It does suggest the need to be realistic in our assessments—particularly with respect to understanding the negative consequences of our sins. So how do we find the right balance and avoid being either overly optimistic or overly pessimistic? The test suggested by Moroni (Moroni 7:16–17) reviewed in chapter 1 is a good place to start. If we are so worried about making a mistake, or about having made a mistake, that we lose faith in ourselves and our ability to reach our eternal goals, we need to let the light in. If we are so optimistic (overconfident) that we fail to see the need for Christ in our lives or we make decisions that put our faith at risk, we need to start facing reality.

Chapter summary

The scriptural imperative to establish a positive frame of reference, balanced with a concern about planning, preparation, and avoiding sin, provides an important foundation for emotional and mental health. Following are several questions we can ask ourselves as an indication of whether we need to work on letting in more light.

1. Do I tend to focus on what's wrong rather than what's right about myself and others?
2. Do I tend to focus on what's wrong rather than what's right about situations I find myself in?
3. Do I analyze things to the point that all I see are the negatives?
4. Do I ask too many of the unanswerable "why" questions

about myself or problems in my life?

5. Am I so optimistic in attitude that I fail to plan properly for difficulties, or make unhealthy choices, without considering carefully the consequences?

As discussed in this chapter, there is great value in having a positive frame of reference as a way of smoothing out the bumps in life. President Hinckley said it this way: "I am asking that we stop seeking out the storms and enjoy more fully the sunlight. I am suggesting that as we go through life we 'accentuate the positive.' I am asking that we look a little deeper for the good."[3] Another rather amazing tool that will help us have better emotional and mental health is the power of forgiveness described in the next chapter.

Notes

1. Address delivered 18 June 1983 at BYU—Hawaii.
2. Neal A. Maxwell, "Apply the Atoning Blood of Christ," *Ensign*, Nov. 1997, 22).
3. Gordon B. Hinckley, *Faith: The Essence of True Religion* (Salt Lake City: Deseret Book, 1989), 74.

5 The amazing power of forgiveness

FORGIVENESS IS AN AMAZINGLY POWERFUL tool in helping us improve our emotional and mental health. Forgiveness can be as effective in eliminating emotional pain as is aspirin, or other analgesic medications, in controlling physical pain. It can help us combat emotional and mental disorders in the same way that antibiotics are so helpful in fighting infection. Pain resulting from abuse, deception, betrayal, humiliation, rejection, or any number of other offenses that we commonly experience in this life is often dealt with in counterproductive ways. Some resort to overuse of legal medications, and others resort to using illegal drugs. Some build walls around themselves or fill their lives with empty distractions. Some push limits, eat too much, try to get even with whoever has offended them, or keep repeating mistakes from the past. Others follow the direction of scripture and learn to forgive. Those who forgive are the only ones who find the permanent relief they seek.

Instructions to forgive and examples of forgiveness are found throughout scripture and cover all ages of time. It's a very old and ageless principle. Yet modern researchers and health professionals are just now coming on board. A relatively large body of research is building that indicates the value of forgiveness in reducing depression and increasing self-confidence, vitality, and hope. Forgiveness has been shown to improve relationships, and it is correlated with fewer health problems and a lower incidence of the most serious illnesses. Training programs focusing on forgiveness have been shown to be helpful in drug and alcohol treatment programs, criminal rehabilitation programs, and anger management training. And to think, this miracle therapy, available to anyone without costly clinical interventions, has been available since the beginning of time.

Forgiveness in scripture

One of the earliest examples of forgiveness in scripture is also one of the best. Joseph in the Old Testament suffered at the hands of his brothers in a way that few of us are called on to endure. As a youth, Joseph was hated by his brothers, who were jealous of his favored relationship with their father. Ultimately this hatred led Joseph's brothers to plot his death, although the plan was modified at the last moment and Joseph was instead sold into slavery. Joseph was a victim in the extreme in that he suffered abandonment, betrayal, humiliation, lost opportunity, and years of struggle. As you remember the story, after many years of suffering, Joseph gained a position of authority in Egypt, and through a series of events, his brothers found themselves at his mercy.

Joseph might have been full of bitterness and anger after so many years, and he might have relished the opportunity he now had to make his brothers suffer as he had. But to his brothers he said, "Now therefore fear ye not: I will nourish you, and your little ones. And he comforted them, and spake kindly unto them" (Genesis 50:21). Somehow Joseph had been able to follow the imperative of scripture and forgive even serious sin. Imagine the emotional benefit to Joseph and the value of his forgiveness to his family.

During the Lord's mortal ministry, Peter came to him on one occasion and asked how often we should forgive an offense. Peter asked if perhaps seven times might be the magic number. The Lord's answer was, "I say not unto thee, Until seven times: but, Until seventy times seven" (Matthew 18:21–22). Also in the New Testament, the Lord said, "But if ye forgive not men their trespasses, neither will your Father forgive your trespasses" (Matthew 6:15). In this dispensation, the Lord taught: "My disciples, in days of old, sought occasion against one another and forgave not one another in their hearts; and for this evil they were afflicted and sorely chastened. Wherefore, I say unto you, that ye ought to forgive one another; for he that forgiveth not his brother his trespasses standeth condemned before the Lord; for there remaineth in him the greater sin. I, the Lord, will forgive whom I will forgive, but of you it is required to forgive all men" (D&C 64:8–10).

When taken together, these scriptures suggest that we need to be continually forgiving, no matter how often we are offended. We are to forgive all offenses whether they be major or minor, and we need to forgive whether or not the offender apologizes or deserves our forgiveness. It's also clear from these scriptures that there are significant consequences when we fail to do so. Even the faithful in former times, the disciples, were afflicted and sorely chastened when they failed to forgive. Not only that, but they couldn't be forgiven of their sins as long as they were unwilling to forgive others.

The wording of these scriptures puts them in the form of a challenge—almost like forgiveness is a requirement of discipleship that we must meet in order to please God or to avoid His punishment. Undoubtedly, forgiveness is a requirement of discipleship, but I expect that the Lord's primary concern is for our welfare. The fact that our sins won't be forgiven unless we forgive others isn't an arbitrary condition established by the Lord to test our character. It's an inevitable consequence of our unforgiving thoughts and actions. Since God can't change those thoughts and actions for us without violating our agency, the consequences of failing to forgive can't be removed until we voluntarily make changes in ourselves.

As a side note regarding the last scripture cited above, it can be confusing to understand what the Lord meant when he said that our failing to forgive is a worse sin than the sin of the person we fail to forgive. The sin against us may be more serious if compared to a list of all sins in order of magnitude; but we are not accountable for that sin, and it will hurt us on into the future only if we fail to forgive. That makes our failing to forgive the greater sin in the sense that it's the only one that will continue to cause us pain over time and the only sin in the given situation for which we are responsible.

What is forgiveness?

There are three basic elements of forgiveness:

How we act

How do we behave in our relationships with those who offend us? To be forgiving in our actions means to avoid trying to get even. It means treating the other person well in spite of how we have been treated.

How we feel

How do we feel when thinking about or when in the presence of someone who has offended us? To forgive at an emotional level means that we can think about or be in the presence of those who have offended us without becoming angry, hurt, or defensive.

How we think

What do we think of those who have offended us? To truly forgive means to hope the best for that person rather than thinking evil of the offender. It means to focus on the positive and not the negative aspects of those who offend us.

We haven't forgiven until we have satisfied all three conditions. Mary, in an earlier example, was divorced by her husband, who left her and their five children for another woman. For some time, Mary had problems with her former husband on all three levels suggested above. First, she very much wanted to get even. In an effort to make certain that everyone knew what a scoundrel he was, she said negative things about her former husband to their children, her friends, and her family. She put pressure on her bishop and stake president to excommunicate him. She sent her former husband nasty notes and did whatever she could to limit his access to their children. She rationalized much of her behavior, such as convincing herself that she was protecting her children by limiting their exposure to such an evil person. But the truth is that her basic motivation was the desire to get even with him in any way that she could.

At an emotional level, Mary couldn't think about her former husband or be in his presence without considerable pain. She experienced a tangle of emotion, including anger, fear, jealousy, loss, and personal hurt whenever he called to discuss a family issue. Potentially wonderful family activities like the baptism of their eight-year-old were horrible for Mary because of the emotional dynamic. It was also extremely painful when she would hear what had once been their favorite song on the radio or when a car would drive by similar to the one he drove. This was all bad enough, but she suffered even more when her former husband's new wife entered the picture. On top of everything else, Mary became anxious and self-conscious whenever the new wife was around.

At a cognitive level, Mary was consumed with negative thoughts about her predicament and how much she hated her former husband for what he had done. She hoped, frankly, that he would suffer endless torment, and she hoped for something even worse for his new wife. She imagined and hoped for his business to fail or for him to contract some incurable disease. She emphasized all of his negatives in her mind and failed to see anything positive.

The consequences of Mary's failing to forgive are obvious. The personal pain was substantial and triggered periods of depression and anxiety. She lost spiritual communication at those times, and her relationships with others suffered. Her children resented her negative comments about their father, and they were upset by her efforts to keep them from seeing him. Her friends and family grew weary of her complaints and increasingly found it uncomfortable to be around Mary. Even worse, as long as Mary insisted on thinking and acting as she did, the Lord could do nothing to relieve her emotional burden. That burden resulted naturally from her choices, which the Lord could not overrule. In terms of the scripture cited previously, it's easy to see that the problems Mary brought on herself were worse than those resulting directly from her former husband's infidelity. In that sense, even though adultery is technically a much greater sin, her failing to forgive was the greater mistake in terms of its impact on Mary.

What forgiveness is not

The forgoing is meant to define what forgiveness is, but it might also help to define what it is not. Several common assumptions about forgiveness can be misleading. For example:

Forgiveness is not forgetting

Not only is it unnecessary to forget in order to forgive an offense, it's not even possible. Research suggests that once intense emotion is encoded or classically conditioned, it is virtually indelible. The memory may be deactivated, but it won't disappear—at least not from a biochemical standpoint. Also, speaking philosophically, forgiveness is an active process. It requires us to decide to let an offense go emotionally—something we can't do if we are no longer aware of it. When the Lord said, "I will forgive their iniquity, and I will remember their sin no more" (Jeremiah 31:34), He didn't promise amnesia. Rather, the sin no longer counts with God. It's no doubt remembered, but God will act toward us as if it had been forgotten. Likewise, when we forgive, we may remember the offense, but we no longer harbor ill will or suffer from it emotionally. In that sense, it's as if it had been forgotten.

Saying this in another way, we must remember in order to forgive. On the opposite side of the coin, it's also important to forgive before we forget. Issues surrounding repressed memory are not clearly understood, but there is reason to believe that particularly painful experiences are sometimes suppressed from conscious thought. When that happens, a person is not free from the effects of the offense, nor do they truly forget. They simply avoid dealing with the issue consciously, and they may experience problems related to the offense that are difficult to address since the actual cause for their distress is suppressed. In other words, the arousal areas of our brain may be activated, causing emotional and even physical problems, while the conscious part of our brain is denying that there is a problem in the first place. An example of this would be someone who claims not to be angry about an offense and who says that the offender has been completely forgiven, when the issue is still very much alive at a pre-conscious level.

Because of the way our brain operates, I'm not aware of anyone who has the capacity to forget on command. There are some who have the emotional advantage of being quicker to forget than others, but I doubt that there is anyone who can turn off memory at will. Offenses once forgiven will disappear from active memory, and those of lesser consequence may even be forgotten with time, but this process occurs naturally and safely after forgiveness, not before.

Forgiveness is not tolerance

To forgive an offense is not the equivalent of tolerating it. It's sometimes necessary to forgive on one hand and to take action to protect oneself or to see justice served on the other. For instance, if your child is molested, your emotional and mental health depends on forgiving the offender. This involves the three basic factors addressed earlier. You need to avoid the temptation to get even or to hurt the offender. You must get to the point where you are not emotionally troubled when thinking about or being in the presence of the offender. And you need to have the offender's best interest at heart. At the same time, it's important to alert authorities about the offense and to protect your children. You certainly don't act as if nothing had happened, or assume repentance on the offender's part and again put your children at risk. Even though it might affect the offender's reputation, you would also not hesitate to warn others who might be in danger. This can all be done without sacrificing forgiveness in the process.

As additional examples, assume that someone defrauds you financially. You can certainly forgive and yet never again trust that person with your funds. You can forgive a friend who has deeply hurt you without regaining the close relationship that you once enjoyed. You can forgive a spouse for infidelity or some other serious offense and still file for divorce in order to protect yourself and your children. You can also forgive a former spouse without becoming good friends or developing a warm relationship in the process. Boundaries are sometimes important, and the consequences of the offense may continue at some level even after forgiveness. But the pain is gone. The interest in vengeance is gone, and you no longer harbor ill will. In short, you don't have to tolerate what people do just because you forgive them for doing it.

Forgiveness is not excusing

It's not necessary to forgive a behavior that can be excused—meaning a behavior that is clearly beyond a person's control. For instance, parents of a schizophrenic don't need to forgive mean-spirited or strange comments if they understand that their child is ill and cannot control such outbursts. You don't need to forgive the rude intrusion of someone who bumps into you in line if you understand that the person is blind. It's not necessary to forgive being ignored by someone when you come to understand that the person didn't actually see you in the first place.

Excusing is easier than forgiving. It simply requires the proper insight, and the negative emotion tends to melt away. For that reason, it's always healthy to look for reasons to legitimately excuse offenses. I remember hearing a story in a Church meeting about how the speaker was offended by the rude, out-of-control behavior of some children on a subway in New York City. He finally said something to the father of the children who had been basically ignoring their behavior. When confronted, the father apologized, saying that he and his children were on the way home from the hospital, where his wife had just died. The children's behavior, and that of their father, was obviously excusable under the the circumstances, and this insight resulted in a dramatic and sudden change in this individual's feelings. Forgiveness was then unnecessary.

Forgiveness is reserved for those cases in which the offensive behavior is the clear result of a person's choice. In other words, we need to forgive whenever there is someone to blame. Of course, that someone isn't necessarily the one committing the offense. Some parents may excuse the behavior of their schizophrenic child but blame God for the fact that the problem exists in the first place. Some may excuse the behavior of an out-of-control child but blame the parents. Forgiveness is a requirement in order to find emotional resolution whenever we place blame on anyone or anything.

Forgiveness is not absolution

Some find it hard to forgive because they equate forgiveness with absolution. They think, "If I forgive him, I am letting him get away with it." Such thinking misses the point made emphatically in scripture that justice is certain at the end of the day. As Paul said in the New Testament, "Recompense to no man evil for evil. Provide things honest in the sight of all men. If it be possible, as much as lieth in you, live peaceably with all men; Dearly beloved, avenge not yourselves, but rather give place unto wrath: for it is written, Vengeance is mine; I will repay, saith the Lord" (Romans 12:17–19). Forgiveness is healing balm to the one forgiving, but it in no way absolves an offender of the consequences of his actions. As the scriptures make clear, absolution comes only after repentance and only through the Atonement of Jesus Christ.

Why is forgiveness so important?

For most of us, this question has an obvious answer. Vicariously or personally, we have all had experience with the debilitating effects on emotional and mental health when grudges, bitter feelings, and hate take over the soul. It's not a pretty picture. Energy is wasted, spirituality is destroyed, and a range of emotional and interpersonal problems ensue. Essentially, an unforgiving person becomes a multiple victim. He or she is victimized in the first instance by the original offense. Then their pain is multiplied by their unhealthy response to the offense. Worse, their failing to forgive traps them and locks them in misery by blocking the only viable means to relief.

Andy experienced what it means to be a multiple victim. Andy prided himself on how well he kept up the things he owned and how he had worked hard to provide a nice home for his family. On returning home from work one evening, he had an uncomfortable feeling that something was wrong, followed almost immediately by a sick feeling in his stomach as he realized that his home had been burglarized. He was a victim. His home had been violated and his possessions unfairly taken.

When Andy surveyed his loss, he became so angry that he slammed his fist into the wall. Two new problems had just been created. There was now an unsightly hole in the wall that he would have to patch, and his hand hurt. In his anger, Andy yelled at his wife on her return home, blaming her for apparently not setting the alarm—again. His wife naturally took offense at his anger and at his insinuation that the burglary was somehow her fault. Now the marriage relationship was strained. Andy suspected (wrongly) that the thieves were two or three young adults who had a bad reputation in the neighborhood. Andy unwisely confronted one of these suspects, who didn't take kindly to Andy's accusations. An argument followed, and some punches were thrown. In the process Andy seriously injured the young man. Now Andy faced legal costs and consequences in addition to everything else.

In the beginning, Andy was an innocent victim of someone else's immorality. That was bad, entailing as it did financial loss and inconvenience, plus the discomfort involved in having one's personal space violated. But his subsequent actions obviously compounded his problems and made him a multiple victim. The anger itself, and the unwise behavior in response to his anger, cost Andy much more than the original offense. Andy was a victim of burglary through no fault of his own, but he was solely responsible for the fact that he was a multiple victim.

Andy understood this at some level, but he tended to blame all of his troubles on the thief. After all, none of this would have happened if he hadn't been robbed. As a result, his anger toward the unknown thief grew and deepened. And, by not assuming responsibility for his actions, he was at the mercy of the situation. Andy's emotions were in effect controlled by events that he could not change and over which he had no control. Think of how much grief Andy could have avoided if he had followed the instruction in scripture to forgive. In this case that might have been more difficult than in some others because the thief remained unknown. There was no explicit person to forgive in this instance. Likewise, there was no apology forthcoming and no sense of justice being served as the thief was sent off to prison. But the opportunity to forgive was still there. Andy ended up suffering greatly when a perfect healing opportunity was within his reach.

Forgiving the small things

If it hasn't happened already, most of us will be the victim of abuse, adultery, robbery, violence, betrayal, or some other major offense. When that happens, as hard as it might be, forgiveness is the quickest and best avenue to emotional resolution. Usually, in fact, it's the only viable way to find emotional peace. But in between the big things are the countless little offenses that come up on a daily basis—mostly within our families and close relationships. Your husband makes a critical comment. Your wife fails to do something important. Your daughter is in an emotional funk. Your son fails to do the chore he had promised to complete before he went off with his friends. The employee you count on drops the ball. Your boss blames you for a problem that was not your fault. Your good friend forgets your birthday.

Unless we are in a coma or living alone in a cave somewhere, there is hardly a day that goes by without some minor offense coming our way, which means that we all have many opportunities to forgive. Those who have an unforgiving heart certainly can't blame the fact on insufficient opportunity to practice. By forgiving the small things, we prepare ourselves to better deal with the big ones. We also avoid the stress from constant irritation caused by everyday issues that plague so many of us. Forgiving the small things is also one of those essential requirements of success in marriage and family life, or in any close relationship.[1]

What gets in the way of forgiving?

Most good people understand the need to forgive others, but they find it to be like so many other virtues—much easier to talk about than to do. Following are several factors that often get in the way. Understanding these common obstacles can help us be more forgiving.

Some get caught in victim status

Andy, in an earlier example, made the common mistake of blaming the offender for the emotional impact of the offense. In truth, it wasn't the burglary per se that caused Andy's anger, but rather what Andy chose to think in the situation that caused him to be so upset. Andy kept thinking how unfair it was and how violated he felt. He thought things like, *I don't have time to deal with this*, and *It's going to cost me a ton to recover*. When he thought he knew who the thief was, he thought, *I'm not going to let him get away with it*. Obsessively thinking these kinds of thoughts fueled Andy's anger. His upset may be understandable in the sense that many victims dwell on their loss and seek to get even. But it's critical to understand that this normal response isn't automatic or necessary. When we understand that the emotional impact when victimized is potentially within our control, we have taken the first step to forgiveness. The process begins by believing that it's possible.

Like Andy, some people remain emotional victims because they blame the offender rather than accepting responsibility for their own pain.

Others remain victims because they depend on their victim status to justify other problems that they might have. A divorced mother, for instance, may use the fact of her divorce to explain away character flaws. She might say, "This explains why I yell at my kids," or "Everything would be going well in my life if he hadn't done this to me." Rather than be honest with ourselves, many of us use our trials to justify our shortcomings. Whenever there is an emotional payoff for remaining a victim, we are obviously less motivated to forgive and move on.

Others get stuck as victims because of the illusion that by not forgiving, they are less likely to be hurt again. This is often true in victims of some form of infidelity. Rather than forgive the offense, they keep the offense alive in their mind and become hyper-vigilant and suspicious. They are afraid to do otherwise, thinking that they will just get hurt again if they are not careful. In actuality, suspicion and failing to forgive increases the chance of a partner hurting us again. As long as we make the decision to stay in a relationship, we have no choice but to assume that things will work out. If we are disappointed, we can deal with it. If we are suspicious and untrusting, we increase the chance of disaster in our relationship while bringing on ourselves all of the negative consequences of failing to forgive

Some are afraid to let the other person get away with it

Forgiving is sometimes perceived as an act of weakness that undermines personal integrity and sends the wrong message to the offender. Thoughts underlying this perception include, "If I forgive, he will think he has gotten away with it." "If I forgive, he won't understand how wrong he is." "If I give an inch, he will just take a mile." "I'm a fool for not seeing the offense coming. I would be an even bigger fool if I let it happen again." Thinking in these ways effectively blocks motivation to forgive and is a common reason that good people find themselves unable to forgive.

Christine is an example of someone stuck in this position. Her husband had a spending problem. He was a financial consultant and believed that in order to be successful in his business he had to present the appearance of prosperity. As a result, he frequently spent money the family could not really afford on new cars, clothes, and other things that Christine believed to be unnecessary. Aggravating the problem, it seemed like whenever Christine wanted to buy something for herself or their children, her husband always complained that there wasn't enough money. This problem came up regularly in one form or another, which presented Christine with ongoing frustration. But an even bigger issue surfaced when Christine discovered that her husband had been signing her name to various legal documents without her knowledge—documents that committed the family to financial liabilities and threatened their financial security.

Christine understood the requirement to forgive, but she found that to be very difficult for the reasons outlined previously. If she didn't complain about her husband's decisions, she believed that he would just do more of the same. She also felt obligated to get him to see the light before he ruined the family financially. Furthermore, she criticized herself for not being more aware and on top of things, and she felt foolish for letting things get to the point they had. Christine also found it hard to forgive an offense that kept coming up over and over again. It seemed more difficult to forgive with each repetition.

Christine fretted and obsessed over this problem and often flew into a rage when another incident surfaced. She resented her husband and found it virtually impossible to feel or act warmly toward him. She suffered virtually all of the common consequences of failing to forgive including reduced spirituality, health issues, and relationship problems. But what were her options? Could she safely forgive in this situation, and if she did so, what would that entail?

Based on the previous discussion, forgiving her husband would need to occur on three levels. She would need to quit yelling at him and quit trying to make him pay for what he was doing to their marriage and family. She would need to get to the point where she could be in control emotionally when dealing with her husband about this issue. Last, she would need to think the best of her husband and dwell on his positives rather than his negatives. All of this would be difficult, but theoretically possible. And it would be a lot more likely to happen if Christine understood that she could do all of this while still taking a stand on the issue that troubled her. She could still speak her mind regarding her husband's financial decisions, but without rancor, bitterness, and lecturing. (Ideas about how to do this in conflict situations will be given in a later chapter.) Christine could also take steps to protect herself and her family from her husband's poor decisions. As a last resort, she could even lay down ultimatums and eventually file for divorce if directed by the Spirit to do so.

This last option would naturally be appropriate only in extreme situations and as led by the Spirit. Fortunately, with a forgiving attitude, Christine would be in a better position to receive the spiritual guidance she needed. She would also be in a much stronger position to influence her husband to change his ways. Without forgiveness, her bitterness and anger tended to force her husband away. If she approached him with a forgiving and more loving attitude, he would be much more likely to listen.

You might think that a balanced approach as described here, which includes forgiveness, would be hard to achieve. And you would be right. On the other hand, it would be a lot less painful and infinitely more effective than Christine's initial counterproductive responses.

It's hard to forgive if we insist on fairness

A final obstacle to forgiveness is the common tendency to insist on fairness. We want to see justice done. A form of righteous indignation wells up, and we find it difficult to make the truly righteous choice to forgive. In addition to the reasons outlined above, Christine in the previous example found it hard to forgive because she wanted fairness. Several aspects of her situation were certainly unfair.

Christine was fiscally responsible and tried hard to live within the family budget. It wasn't fair that her husband didn't do his part. Obviously it wasn't fair of her husband to commit her to financial liabilities without her knowledge or approval. She would certainly never do something like that to him. It wasn't fair when bill collectors called, pressuring Christine about debts that she knew nothing about or had done nothing to incur. Nor was it fair that her husband bought so many things for himself when she didn't have the same opportunity. And then he even had the gall to complain about some of her expenditures. Last, it wasn't fair that her husband rationalized his behavior and refused to accept responsibility or apologize for how it affected Christine.

Given all that was unjust in this situation, there is no way that Christine could forgive her husband as long as she insisted on fairness. Hers was like most situations in that forgiveness typically requires us to endure something that just isn't fair. But the fact is that failing to forgive multiplies the unfairness in any situation. By not forgiving, we make a bad situation worse. We compound the pain that is inevitable in hurtful situations, and we block the quickest way to emotional resolution.

Chapter summary

In requiring us to forgive, the Lord has done us a huge favor. Forgiveness is an amazingly powerful tool in improving our emotional and mental health. Following are some questions that we can ask ourselves that may reveal the need to forgive or obstacles to forgiving others.

1. Is there someone in my life I hate, or someone with whom I am trying to get even?
2. Do I get anxious, angry, or emotionally uncomfortable when I think about, or when I am in the presence of, an offender?
3. Is there an enemy that I obsess about, think evil of, and about whom I think primarily negatives?
4. Do I believe that I must forget in order to truly forgive?
5. Do I believe that I am tolerating unacceptable behavior if I forgive an offense?
6. Am I frequently frustrated by offenses that come up on a daily basis?
7. Do I blame the offense or the offender rather than accepting responsibility for my pain?
8. Can I let an offender get away with sin and leave justice to the Lord?
9. Can I accept something that isn't fair without letting it upset me?

Most of us have room to improve our ability to forgive others. Removing some of the obstacles to forgiveness as outlined above is a good place to start. There are also other steps we can take to this end that are outlined in the next chapter. Here the impact of anger on our emotional and mental health is discussed. The same things that we can do to manage anger in our lives will also help us forgive others. Finally, to complete a discussion of forgiveness, the great value in forgiving ourselves, as well as forgiving others, must be considered. This will also be discussed in a subsequent chapter.

Note
1. See one of my earlier works, *Sacred Union* (Salt Lake City: Deseret Book, 1999).

6 Unload anger

ANGER IS A SUBJECT CLOSELY associated with forgiveness. The negative consequences of unhealthy anger are similar to the consequences of failing to forgive, and the steps we can take to be a more forgiving person will help us manage anger. Like forgiveness, the scriptures also have a lot to say about anger. God knows how important it is that we manage this emotion productively. Otherwise, our spirituality suffers, interpersonal relationships can be ruined, and our emotional, mental, and even physical health may be compromised.

It should be pointed out, however, that these unwanted consequences apply only to the negative expression of anger. Experiencing angry feelings when we are offended is natural. In fact, the arousal centers of the brain seem to fire automatically. Therefore, some level of discomfort when we are hurt or offended is inevitable and healthy. Anger can help us assertively deal with difficult situations, and it may encourage our taking reasonable steps to protect ourselves and others from future harm. On the other hand, we are all familiar with how anger can get out of control. The good news is that the centers of emotion in the brain that fire automatically to create feelings of anger exist in a feedback loop with the pre-frontal cortex or the conscious part of the brain. Whether or not the arousal centers continue a stress reaction depends on input from our conscious self. The anger will either subside or be intensified, depending on our thoughts.

It's most likely that this is the point at which temptation enters the picture. Either through evil influence, or our own poor thought habits, many of us think in ways that intensify and prolong anger. When we do so, intensified anger places the body under unnecessary stress and increases the chances of counterproductive behavior. It's this intensified anger and any associated unhealthy behavior that the Lord warns about in scripture. The basic emotion itself is not the problem. In fact, it's important to first recognize feelings of anger in order to manage them. In that sense, being afraid of anger to the point of denying its existence may interfere with the opportunity we have to control the emotion.

This can happen to those who believe that all feelings of anger are sinful and deny such feelings in themselves even though they are angry. It can also be true of people mistreated as children who have a conditioned fear of expressing anger. In either case, it's important to first accept our natural emotional responses and then manage them.

Anger in the scriptures

In several places the scriptures talk about God's anger directed toward evil and unrighteousness. For instance, in Doctrine and Covenants 5:8, the Lord said, "Oh, this unbelieving and stiff-necked generation—mine anger is kindled against them." As another example of godly anger, there is the well-known instance in which Jesus made a scourge of small cords and drove moneychangers from the temple (see John 2:13–17). The Lord was displeased with the manner in which His Father's house had been made into a "den of thieves," and that displeasure was expressed dramatically. Based on these scriptures, it's obvious that anger ultimately has a positive form and expression.

When it comes to mortals, however, anger is typically characterized in scripture as something evil—something that must be controlled or eliminated. Human anger is described as a curse (see Genesis 49:7) or as foolish (see Proverbs 14:17). Also in Proverbs, anger is described as cruel and outrageous (see Proverbs 27:4). Elsewhere in scripture we are advised to put off or put away anger (see Colossians 3:8 and Ephesians 4:31). In several places, anger is referred to as something instigated by Satan. The Lord Himself said, "For verily, verily I say unto you, he that hath the spirit of contention is not of me, but is of the devil, who is the father of contention, and he stirreth up the hearts of men to contend with anger, one with another. Behold, this is not my doctrine, to stir up the hearts of men with anger, one against another; but this is my doctrine, that such things should be done away" (3 Nephi 11:29–30).

These warnings about anger obviously make sense given the tendency we mortals have to intensify anger and to engage in counterproductive behavior as a result of its influence. It's also often true that our anger results from unrighteous judgments, attempts to control someone else, or from self-centeredness in various forms. In that sense, negative anger originates in sinful thought or intent. Of course, once in a state of intensified anger, a person will then likely make unrighteous judgments, try to control another, or act in a destructive and self-centered way. When so motivated, the expression of anger is sinful. No wonder Jesus would say that anger, as we mortals commonly experience it, is of the devil and not of God. No wonder that He would later say, "Whosoever is angry with his brother shall be in danger of his judgment. And whosoever shall say to his brother, Raca, shall be in danger of the council; and whosoever shall say, Thou fool, shall be in danger of hell fire" (3 Nephi 12:22).

Clearly we learn from scripture that anger is to be managed and eliminated in its negative expression. Our example is that of the Savior, who was falsely accused, mocked, and railed against, but who stood completely composed before Pontius Pilate and others. When mightily provoked, He did not respond in anger, nor was there a seething "just-you-wait" undertone as He majestically endured His tormenters. As difficult as it might be in some situations, this is obviously the example that should direct and motivate us. Imagine what the world would be like if we all followed this example. There would be happier families and neighborhoods and fewer problems between nations, and conflicts could be easily solved. Child abuse, divorce, and violent crimes would be greatly reduced or eliminated. There would also be great benefits to each of us individually in the form of improved emotional, mental, and physical health.

Do I have an anger problem?

With some people, it's completely obvious that they have an anger problem. These are those who slam doors, shout, and intimidate. These are people who put their fists through walls in anger, chase after people on the freeway who have offended them, and abuse their loved ones. Others have an equally debilitating but less obvious anger problem. They seethe quietly, withdrawing in self-pity, and react in passive but aggressive ways. These are people who undermine those with whom they are angry, but usually without direct confrontation. These are often bitter and negative people who blame others for their problems. They may threaten suicide, promise but fail to follow through with assignments, or withdraw from relationships without explanation. Whether directly or indirectly expressed, this kind of anger subverts health and upsets relationships.

Following is a checklist of items that can help identify an anger problem of either the overt or less obvious variety. Make a check in front of any item that is true of you.

___ I realize that I have a quick temper.

___ I have broken something or hurt myself or someone else in anger.

___ I often find myself slowly stewing over daily irritants.

___ People, especially family members, stay out of my way when I'm in one of my moods.

___ I give the silent treatment when someone upsets me.

___ I'm known for using sarcasm when expressing humor.

___ I may not show it, but I seethe inside when people disagree with me.

___ I can't stand it when other people do stupid things.

___ People know that they aren't going to get away with hurting me or someone I love.

___ Although I know I shouldn't, I tend to blame others for my problems.

___ I'm known for telling the brutal truth whether it hurts people or not.

___ I'm a lot less patient than I would like to be.

___ I often go out of my way to avoid confronting someone who has hurt me.

___ I don't easily forget when someone does me wrong.

___ I say or do embarrassing things when I get angry.

___ When I'm upset, I will sometimes avoid doing things I know I should do.

___ I can get very upset about something and later not even remember what I was upset about.

___ People generally disappoint me.

___ I frequently say or do things in anger that I later regret.

___ I know I shouldn't say anything, but sooner or later it spills out.

___ I believe I have to stand my ground or people will walk all over me.

___ Someone reading this book asked me to take this anger inventory.

The last item on this checklist is included somewhat facetiously, but the truth is that we can often get important clues about our problems from those close to us. If a good friend or family member suggests, in whatever way, that you have an anger problem, the shoe might fit. This list is also included here to be thought provoking, not to identify a character flaw in any scientific way. If any item is true of you, it indicates an area where you might benefit from adjusting your thinking. If several items are true of you, it suggests the need to read on carefully. You will likely benefit from one or more of the steps in managing anger described below.

General principles and anger management

Before listing a few specific anger management tools, it's important to consider basic principles that can help us handle conflict situations without undue anger. Joseph Smith was once asked how he was able to govern the community of Saints as effectively as he did. His response was, "I teach them correct principles and they govern themselves."[1] This same truth applies with respect to self-management. When we operate on the basis of correct principles in our personal life, we naturally think in ways that minimize unhealthy and maximize healthy emotion. It's then much easier to avoid the kind of thinking that builds anger and resentment. When we are living by certain principles, handling even difficult situations without unhealthy emotion is much easier.

Not surprisingly, the scriptures are the best place to find the principles that relate to controlling anger. Humility, as taught in many places in scripture, is certainly one of those ideals. Unhealthy anger commonly results when we have to be right about something or when we insist that our opinion be respected, but that doesn't happen. This was the problem when Joy and her husband were driving to visit friends. Joy, for the umpteenth time in their marriage, complained that her husband was driving too fast and that he was following other cars too closely. She also insisted that they were taking the long way and that if her husband had simply turned off and followed a different route, they would have arrived at their destination long ago.

Joy's husband saw nothing wrong with his driving, and he was convinced that he knew the best way to get to their friend's house. He blew up at his wife's suggestions and called her some unflattering names. Joy's husband was naturally irritated by his wife's backseat driving. But it went beyond irritation to unhealthy anger. He could blame his initial discomfort on his wife's critical and picky comments, but he couldn't blame her for his intense anger. That resulted from his insistence on doing things his way and from his requirement that his wife accept his choices without complaint. This wouldn't have happened if he had been sufficiently humble.

Joy's husband had several options available in dealing with his wife's complaints. He might have simply commented on her backseat driving and asked for her cooperation without name calling and without getting intensely angry in the process. This would most likely be the response if he recognized his initial irritation but then managed it so that it did not intensify and get out of hand. With enough humility, he might even have backed off on his speed a little or put a little more distance between cars out of consideration for his wife's concerns. Furthermore, he could have given his wife the satisfaction of considering her opinion regarding the route of travel, whether or not he agreed with it. Reactions like these would have gone a long way toward eliminating contention.

For her part, Joy also insisted that she was right, both about her husband's driving and the route he was following. She further insisted that she had a right to her opinion and that she wouldn't allow her husband to speak to her the way he did. In thinking this way, Joy also became very angry. She didn't voice her anger to the extent that her husband did, but she stewed quietly. She would make him pay over time. Lovemaking would be out of the question for the foreseeable future, as would civil conversation for that matter. This incident would be harbored and brought up again and again.

Unhealthy anger, both in the case of Joy and her husband, would have been preventable if humility had entered the equation. With humility, these two would not have demanded respect, nor would either have insisted that he or she was right. That being the case, they may have been irritated with each other, but they would not have experienced the mean-spirited anger that they did. Of course, the principle of forgiveness, discussed in the previous chapter, could have also saved the day. If Joy had forgiven her husband for his sarcastic comments and angry reaction to her suggestions, it would have helped immensely. Or if her husband had forgiven his wife for her backseat driving, an ugly experience would have likewise been avoided. The ideal would be for both husband and wife to be forgiving, but considerable pain would have been avoided if even one of them had practiced this principle.

Along with humility and forgiveness, patience is another general principle that will automatically moderate anger. We get angry when something has to happen and doesn't, or when something that shouldn't happen does. Joy had to have the respect of her husband, and she insisted on having it in the immediate situation. Also, she was not about to allow her husband to mistreat her verbally, and that was an absolute and immediate requirement as well. With more patience, she could have tolerated her husband's imperfections with some level of irritation but without undue anger. There was nothing wrong with her ultimate desire that her husband treat her better. The problem was her timing. Her husband isn't perfect yet, but he is still evolving. If loved and supported, he is likely to mellow with time and grow into the person she wants him to be. With criticism and anger, it's likely to take a lot longer.

Paul in the New Testament taught, "Let us run with patience the race that is set before us" (Hebrews 12:1). In a similar vein, President Joseph F. Smith observed:

> We want things a long time before we get them, and the fact that we wanted them a long time makes them all the more precious when they come. In nature we have our seedtime and harvest; and if children were taught that the desires that they sow may be reaped by and by through patience and labor, they will learn to appreciate whenever a long-looked-for goal has been reached. Nature resists us and keeps admonishing us to wait; indeed, we are compelled to wait.[2]

As in Joy's example, none of us will be nearly as frustrated (and therefore angry) when we learn to be patient. We have to give ourselves and others the time it takes to become what we eventually will be.

Unselfishness is yet another grand principle taught in scripture that dissolves anger before it gets out of control. If Joy's husband had been more focused on his wife's needs rather than his own, he could have slowed down or at least given respect to her opinion without anger. By focusing only on himself ("Why does she insist on telling me how to drive? It makes me crazy when she does that! I can't stand it!"), he became excessively angry and then suffered even more because of his wife's response to his anger. He became a double victim as explained in the preceding chapter.

There are also other principles taught in scripture that will help us manage anger. Charity, compassion, benevolence, and tolerance come to mind as examples. Having a temper, or other emotional control issue for that matter, often grows out of a failure to apply these basic virtues in our lives. This could be part of the reason that the Lord said, "Come unto me, all ye that labour and are heavy laden, and I will give you rest. Take my yoke upon you, and learn of me; for I am meek and lowly in heart: and ye shall find rest unto your souls. For my yoke is easy, and my burden is light" (Matthew 11:28–30). Issues are easier handled and less likely to get emotionally complicated when we do things the Lord's way. In that sense, when we incorporate correct principles in our thinking, life is easier and our emotional and mental health improve.

Anger management tools

Along with doing our best to incorporate basic gospel virtues in how we live our lives, there are a number of specific things we can do to manage anger. For example, we can stop angry thoughts and put our mind somewhere else.

It's difficult, if not impossible, to stop angry emotion directly. We might be successful in biting our tongue or refusing to act in anger, but the emotion itself will continue as long as we continue to think angry thoughts. The good news is that we do have the power to stop angry thinking. That, in turn, will moderate the emotion. The trick involves becoming aware of our thoughts and making the decision to stop any thinking that incites anger. Then it's important to turn our thinking to some other topic altogether. If we stay focused on whatever offended us, even if we are trying to think positively about the incident or the offender, we are likely to slip into negative thought. Putting our mind on some other issue entirely is the best way to avoid this happening.

In summary, the steps toward emotional resolution when offended are:

1. Recognize that we are thinking in ways that are causing our anger to intensify.
2. Decide to stop it. Tell ourself, "I'm not going to go there!"
3. Put our mind somewhere else. Go for a walk, call a friend (to talk about something other than the problem), read a book, attend to a project, or do whatever that will take your mind away from the offending issue.

Some people have trouble following these simple steps because of incorrect assumptions about anger. For one thing, it's common to assume that anger is caused by outside influences. We say things like, "It made me mad" and "He made me mad." If something outside of ourselves is responsible for our anger, then the release of anger would depend on outside factors as well. And on the surface, it does seem to be that way. For one thing, as suggested earlier, our brains respond with emotion in stressful situations automatically. We can be in a good mood until offended, and then we are suddenly angry. It's also true that our anger usually relates to a specific incident, and it's obvious that we wouldn't be angry if whatever disturbs us hadn't happened.

The truth is that our conscious brain is in control of the intensity of our anger, how long it lasts, and the behavior that results. Furthermore, the fact that we would not have gotten angry if we hadn't been frustrated doesn't mean that the frustration caused the anger. It's like donuts and dieting. Suppose I am trying to lose a few pounds and my wife buys a dozen of my favorite donuts and leaves them on the counter. Whose fault is it if I cave and eat several of the donuts? I could blame my wife for being insensitive, or even malicious if she intended to set me up, but I couldn't blame her for the fact that I ate the donuts. That would clearly be my choice. Likewise, it would also be my choice if I got angry with my wife for the donut temptation. My response could range from the incident being a non-issue, to something humorous, to something extremely upsetting—all depending on how I choose to think about it. That is actually a liberating idea. Anger is related to the offenses that we experience, but it does not intensify or result in problem behavior without our choice. We can manage the emotion both in terms of how we experience it and how we express it.

Another common but mistaken assumption is that expressing anger is a positive thing. Some see anger as a force that builds within us and will cause damage unless released. Repressed anger is believed by many to cause various emotional and physical problems. Over the years, depression, colitis, ulcers, and being overweight have all been blamed on suppressed anger. There are also those who feel that angry outbursts are a form of honesty. They may say, "I'm not trying to hurt you; I'm just honestly sharing my feelings."

Fortunately, current research generally discredits the old notion that suppressing anger is dangerous. There is good reason to believe that being too angry too often is related to coronary disease and other major health problems, but we now know that the *suppression* of anger does not cause ulcers. Nor is there a link, as once thought, between obesity and repressed anger. Actually, there is no credible evidence of any link between health problems and suppressed anger. Research studies suggesting otherwise are typically flawed in ways that make their results meaningless. Furthermore, it has become less fashionable to think of venting hostile emotions as somehow noble and cathartic. More often, currently, such behavior is labeled as self-centered and destructive—a much more accurate description.

Current thinking is more likely to agree with scripture and the opinion of prophets who have consistently held that anger needs to be managed and controlled. Brigham Young in his own direct and colorful style made the point emphatically. "If you give way to your angry feelings, it sets on fire the whole course of nature . . . and you are then apt to set those on fire who are contending with you. When you feel as though you would burst, tell the old boiler to burst, and just laugh at the temptation to speak evil. If you will continue to do that, you will soon be masters of yourselves able, if not to tame, to control your tongues—able to speak when you ought, and to be silent when you ought."[3]

On another occasion Brigham Young said:

> When evil arises within me let me throw a cloak over it, subdue it instead of acting it out upon the false presumption that I am honest and no hypocrite. Let not thy tongue give utterance to the evil that is in thine heart, but command thy tongue to be silent until good shall prevail over the evil, until thy wrath has passed away and the good spirit shall move thy tongue to blessings and words of kindness. So far I believe in being a hypocrite. This is practical with me. When my feelings are aroused to anger by the ill-doings of others, I hold them as I would hold a wild horse, and I gain the victory. Some think and say that it makes them feel better when they are mad, as they call it, to give vent to their madness in abusive and unbecoming language. This, however, is a mistake. Instead of its making you feel better, it is making bad worse. When you think and say it makes you better you give credit to a falsehood. When the wrath and bitterness of the human heart are moulded into words and hurled with violence at one another, without any check or hindrance, the fire has no sooner expended itself than it is again re-kindled through some trifling course, until the course of nature is set on fire; "and it is set on fire in hell."[4]

It's worth noting that President Young does not suggest that we are condemned for having angry feelings or for being tempted to react angrily. There is a problem only if we give in to that temptation. President Young in the above quotes admitted that he too got angry and was tempted to express that anger in unhealthy ways. But he put effort into resisting the temptation. As suggested earlier, the emotion is not necessarily the problem, but how the emotion is expressed.

Use the magic words, "It doesn't matter"

Anger likely only develops when something important happens that shouldn't or when something important doesn't happen that should. In either case, the issue has to be important to us in order to generate emotion. If we can decide that something simply doesn't matter, anger shrivels and dies. The principle involved may matter, and important issues may be involved, but we can decide that the frustration doesn't matter to us—at least not enough to get upset about. As a general rule of thumb, it's reasonable to assume that something doesn't matter if either of two rules applies:

1. The issue is beyond my control. I might care about the issue, pray about it, and do what is reasonable to resolve the problem. But it does no good to become personally upset about something that I cannot realistically do anything about. Examples include the behavior and attitudes of others who disappoint me, acts of nature, common mistakes that all people are prone to make on occasion simply because they are human, and any other problems that I am powerless to prevent and can't fix once they occur. Most people would dramatically shrink the number of things they get angry about if they applied this one rule.

2. I won't care about it fifty years from now. Most things that are upsetting at the time have no long-term implications unless we react to them in a destructive way. An incident on the freeway, for instance, will soon be forgotten unless we chase after an offending driver and cause an accident in the process. Incidents in our families, no matter how painful at the time, might also look very different given the passage of time. In fact, a couple can have an extensive and very painful argument only to forget in a few days what they were arguing about. As a practical matter, nothing in this life matters that much except those things that will effect us into the eternities to come.

Ask ourselves, "Is it worth the cost?"

Sometimes it helps us avoid intensifying anger when we do a quick cost/benefit analysis. Usually if we simply ask ourselves if our anger is going to benefit us if it gets out of control, the obvious answer is no. If I yell and scream, I may get the attention of others, and they may even go along with me for a time. But if changes are coerced, they tend to be short-lived. I will just have to blow up again and again. By venting anger in a mean-spirited way, I may make it obvious that someone has hurt me, and in that way I'm not letting him or her get away with it. But I'm also not constructively addressing the problem. There are more positive ways to confront offenders as suggested later. In fact, those hurting me might not even get my message if I overreact. They might be so focused on my excessive anger that they fail to acknowledge the fact that they have hurt me in the first place. Or those who have offended me may not care that I have been hurt, or they may even take sadistic pleasure in my pain. If I need people like that to recognize their guilt before I can release anger, I'm in serious trouble.

My anger may give me the feeling that I am in control of the situation and I am not allowing others to treat me poorly. But the truth is that my anger is hurting me and doing nothing to equalize the scales of justice. Vengeance does not solve my problem. My anger may give me a sense of protection from abuse, but the fact is that my anger is more likely to make me a target. In a related way, I may use anger to insulate myself from others—a form of emotional distance. But an emotionally sterile world results. The pain of emotional exile is far worse than whatever pain I am trying to insulate myself against. The cure is certainly worse than the disease.

It seems obvious that there is little benefit and a high cost associated with intense anger and acting out. Of course, I'm not recommending a drawn out philosophical discussion with ourselves every time we are offended. Rather, just ask the question, "Will my getting angry gain me anything?" The answer is self-evident, and sometimes just asking the question is enough to let the issue go. As soon as we stop dwelling on the offense and turn our mind to other issues, the anger abates.

Take a deep breath or two

Simple relaxation exercises help some people deal with anger productively. Deep breathing is an example. Breathe in deeply, hold it, and release. Repeat over several minutes. Count back from one hundred by threes. Put on your favorite music. Tense for several seconds and then relax various muscle groups throughout the body. Do some intense exercise. Go for a walk. Read a good book. Take a bubble bath.

As suggested above, virtually anything that takes our mind away from dwelling on the offense and allows us to move on in our thinking will reduce an angry emotion. Of course, relaxing ourselves when angry, and distracting ourselves, is somewhat counterintuitive. The natural response is to go over the offense in great detail and to imagine what we would like to say to the offender and to visualize all the things we would like to do to that person. The only activity along these lines I have seen work well in some situations is writing a nasty letter that is then torn up. Some have reported that they didn't have much luck moving on until they spent the time to formally put all of their negative thoughts on paper. Then when they burned the paper or threw it away, they were able to let the offense go in their mind. However it gets done, the quicker we can decide to let the offense go and move our mind to more productive issues, the quicker we experience emotional resolution.

Apply the confrontation formula in scripture

Although we generally benefit from letting issues go and letting them not matter so much, that's not always the case. Our overall quality of life, our relationships with others, and our emotional health sometimes benefit from confronting an offense. "Moreover if thy brother shall trespass against thee, go and tell him his fault between thee and him alone: if he shall hear thee, thou hast gained thy brother" (Matthew 18:15). An important clue about when to do this is found in section 121 of the Doctrine and Covenants—which provides arguably the best advice found in scripture regarding confrontational situations.

In section 121 the Lord first talks about how authority must be exercised only on the basis of persuasion, long-suffering, gentleness, meekness, and love unfeigned. If that advice were consistently followed, the opportunity for anger and contention in our families and elsewhere would be greatly reduced. When confrontation or reproving is necessary, we are told, "Reproving betimes with sharpness, when moved upon by the Holy Ghost; and then showing forth afterwards an increase of love toward him whom thou hast reproved, lest he esteem thee to be his enemy" (D&C 121:43).

This advice presupposes a control of anger. Those who act out in anger and are controlling and negative in their responses are not moved upon by the Holy Ghost. This scripture also indicates the need to confront an offender only in certain situations when "moved upon by the Holy Ghost." Sometimes it's helpful to confront an offender, and other times it clearly isn't. The Holy Spirit is available to help us know the difference. When it is appropriate to confront an offense, we can also be directed in how to proceed—again, "as moved upon by the Holy Ghost." In general, any confrontation should occur soon after the offense (betimes), and our point should be made clearly (with sharpness). All of this should take place in the context of love, patience, tolerance, and so forth. Then there should be an increase in the expression of love.

This is an excellent formula when confrontation is appropriate. It will help us manage the immediate emotion when we are offended, but it also helps improve relationships long-term, and it can reduce the probability of further hurt.

Chapter summary

Anger is a natural emotion that occurs automatically when we are offended. When managed properly, it has value in helping us confront difficult situations and in protecting us from further hurt. The problem is that many of us intensify anger, prolong it, and act on it in ways that harm ourselves and others. The scriptures clearly warn of this problem and also offer suggestions regarding how to avoid this possibility

Applying basic gospel virtues in our lives such as humility, forgiveness, patience, unselfishness, and tolerance goes a long way toward helping us think in ways that will eliminate unhealthy anger. There are also a number of specific tools mentioned in scripture that can help us avoid overreacting in anger. Several of these have been reviewed above.

The following personal questions are designed to summarize the points made in this chapter.

1. Do I deny anger when I am offended, or do I recognize angry feelings and then move to manage them?
2. Do I blame others for the extent of my anger, or do I recognize how I intensify and prolong the emotion by how I think about the offense?
3. Do I blame others when I act out in anger, or do I accept the responsibility I have to control my actions?
4. Do I hold anger in and quietly seethe and fume, taking my anger out in passive-aggressive ways?
5. Am I focused on applying basic gospel virtues such as humility, patience, and unselfishness in my life to a greater degree?
6. Have I learned anger management techniques that work for me, and do I apply them on a regular basis?

The steps described in this chapter are also relevant in managing emotion in general. In the next chapter, similar techniques will be described in terms of managing fear. Like anger, fear is a basic, natural emotion that has value in our lives, but it can easily get out of control.

Notes

1. Quoted by John Taylor in *Millennial Star*, 15 Nov. 1851, 339.
2. Joseph F. Smith, *Gospel Doctrine: Selections from the Sermons and Writings of Joseph F. Smith*, 5th ed. (Salt Lake City: Deseret Book, 1939), 298.
3. John A. Widtsoe, *Discourses of Brigham Young* (Salt Lake City: Deseret Book, 1954) 269.
4. *Journal of Discourses*, 26 vols. (London: Latter-day Saints' Book Depot, 1854–86), 11:255.

7 Managing fear

LIKE ANGER, FEAR IS A natural and necessary emotion. My wife appreciates the fact that, even if tempted to do so, I no longer play contact sports because of a fear of what is likely to happen if I do. Although growing up in a generation where it wasn't required, I fasten my seat belt and make sure that small children riding with me are properly secured. Doing so might be motivated as much by fear of a traffic citation as by fear of injury, but the behavior is still beneficial. Some people do courageous things, not because they are brave, but because they are afraid to look cowardly in front of friends and family. Some fight through depression because they are afraid to take their life. Others stay committed to difficult marriages because they are afraid of what others might think, or they are afraid of how divorce will impact their children. Most of us avoid any number of spiritually or physically dangerous behaviors because we are afraid of what might happen if we don't.

In this sense, fear is a beneficial emotion. The automatic alarm response we experience in dangerous situations can literally save us as we jump out of the way of a falling boulder or complete a difficult maneuver in our car just in time to avoid an accident, all without giving our actions any conscious thought until after the event. In a similar way, fear resulting from conscious thoughts can save us from potential spiritual death when we respond to a fear of displeasing God or others we love. In fact, God apparently uses this emotion to our benefit at times. He is on record admitting that forceful words are sometimes used in scripture to make sure that they create the proper respect (fear) in His children. "Again, it is written *eternal damnation*; wherefore it is more express than other scriptures, that it might work upon the hearts of the children of men, altogether for my name's glory" (D&C 19:7; emphasis added).

Among other benefits of fear, fear of failing at something can spur us on to greater effort and help us plan effectively. Some level of worry about what might go wrong is useful in helping us develop solutions to problems ahead of time. By fearing potential problems our children might have, we are more likely to teach them properly and to be aware of problems requiring discipline. Concern about our neighbor might help us be a better friend.

In many ways, fear or worry is beneficial. But it's obvious that there is another side to the coin. Fear can easily get out of control, and it must be managed properly. Intense fear can immobilize us. Unhealthy fear can destroy initiative and strangle effectiveness. Misplaced fear can result in failure to keep the commandments, and it can seriously interfere with interpersonal relationships in our family life and elsewhere. From a mental and emotional health standpoint, unmanaged fear results in anxiety, post-traumatic stress, panic attacks, and phobias. As a matter of fact, it's estimated by the Public Health Service that up to 50 percent of the cases treated by mental health practitioners in the United States involve fear-related issues.

Fear in scripture

Fear as described in scripture also appears as something either positive or negative, depending on its form and expression. References throughout the standard works indicate that fear of God is a good thing—even necessary. (See Luke 1:50, 3 Nephi 4:10, and D&C 76:5, among many others.) Fear, in this sense, means to have respect for God, which then naturally motivates us to keep His commandments. But the emotion of fear as we commonly experience it can immobilize us, contribute to sin, and cause significant spiritual, physical, emotional, and interpersonal damage. It's this kind of fear referenced in a number of scriptures:

> For God hath not given us the spirit of fear; but of power, and of love, and of a sound mind. (2 Timothy 1:7)

> Fear not, for I am with thee, and will bless thee. (Genesis 26:24)

> Therefore, whosoever belongeth to my church need not fear, for such shall inherit the kingdom of heaven. (D&C 10:55)

Therefore, fear not, little flock; do good; let earth and hell combine against you, for if ye are built upon my rock, they cannot prevail. . . . Look unto me in every thought; doubt not, fear not. Behold the wounds which pierced my side, and also the prints of the nails in my hands and feet; be faithful, keep my commandments, and ye shall inherit the kingdom of heaven. Amen. (D&C 6:34–37)

President Gordon B. Hinckley was also speaking about this kind of fear when he said:

Who among us can say that he or she has not felt fear? I know of no one who has been entirely spared. Some, of course, experience fear to a greater degree than do others. Some are able to rise above it quickly, but others are trapped and pulled down by it and even driven to defeat. We suffer from the fear of ridicule, the fear of failure, the fear of loneliness, the fear of ignorance. Some fear the present, some the future. Some carry the burden of sin and would give almost anything to unshackle themselves from those burdens but fear to change their lives. Let us recognize that fear comes not of God, but rather that this gnawing, destructive element comes from the adversary of truth and righteousness. Fear is the antithesis of faith. It is corrosive in its effects, even deadly.[1]

It's encouraging that when the Lord and His prophets speak of debilitating fear, they do more than just warn us. They provide suggestions regarding how to overcome it. Several of these suggestions are reviewed below; but first, a description seems in order concerning how the fear system in the brain works. This description is greatly oversimplified, but it represents a best guess as to what is happening based on current research.

Fear from a neurological standpoint

Stimuli that warn of danger such as noises, nonverbal cues from others, messages in our environment, sudden movements, and so forth are sent through neural pathways to the amygdala in the limbic system in the brain. There the significance of the stimulus is determined and an emotional response triggered. This occurs automatically and instantaneously according to pre-programmed criteria wired in by learning or genetic inheritance. The result is immediate escape behavior and physical responses such as a faster heart rate, increased breathing, and sweating. Information then travels along other neural pathways from the limbic system to the neocortex or thinking part of the brain. This is the part of the brain that reasons, thinks, makes decisions, and is aware of the activities in the brain itself. It's at this point that we are conscious of feeling fear and are able to make conscious decisions about it.

From here, the intensity of the fear response, its length, and what we do in response to it is determined. Interestingly, however, neuroanatomists have shown that the pathways that connect the automatic emotional processing system in the limbic system to the thinking part of the brain are asymmetrical. The pathways from the cortex to the amygdala are considerably weaker than the connections from the amygdala to the cortex. This could explain why it's sometimes so difficult to turn off fear responses consciously. It has also been estimated that perhaps 20 percent of the population is born with a more excitable limbic system. These people may automatically respond with greater intensity to a greater range of stimuli than others. Complicating things further, there is reason to believe that repeated stimulation of the amygdala causes hypersensitivity. In other words, the more we respond in fear, the more sensitive we will become to fear provoking stimuli.

All of this leads to the question of how to manage fear from a neuropsychological standpoint. Except in rare instances in which the limbic system and the neural pathways between limbic system and cortex are damaged, it is possible to control our fear response with the conscious brain. It may be more difficult for some than others, and some may benefit from medication to quiet the autonomic reaction in the brain. Some may also benefit from professional counseling to help in the control process, but it remains possible to manage fear through our thinking. There is also reason to believe that the reverse of the hyper-sensitization process mentioned above also occurs. The more we practice controlling fear, the less sensitized to fearful stimuli we become and the more successful we will be in self-management.

Bottom line: from a neuropsychological standpoint, there is hope. New understanding and therapeutic approaches are adding to existing techniques that have proven helpful in giving people control over their fears. There is, of course, also a cure from the standpoint of scripture. There we find that faith is the answer to fear. Following are several specific faith-related suggestions found in scripture that can help anyone deal more effectively with fear.

Be Prepared

"But if ye are prepared ye shall not fear" (D&C 38:30). This scripture is often understood in a relatively specific sense. If we are prepared for economic reversals with adequate savings, minimal debt, and food storage, we can be free of worry about such possibilities. If we have developed highly marketable skills, we need not worry about employment, or if we have prepared well for a test, or some other difficult challenge, we can be more confident of success. This is obviously true. Being prepared does help us deal with specific fears, but there may also be a more general benefit as well.

In context, the above quotation from D&C 38 talks about being prepared in a spiritual sense through prayer and gospel study (v. 30). It talks about a spiritual endowment (v. 32) that will be given to the faithful and how that spiritual endowment will guarantee the Saints escape from the power of their enemies (v. 31). Trouble from wars in far countries and even from within need not be feared (v. 29). That would include all of the political upheaval, wars, and general wickedness so troubling in our day.

Most of us at one time or another have been tempted to worry as upsetting world or national events come to our attention through a newspaper headline or in some other way. Some become so fearful that they worry about whether to bring children into such a troubled world, and those with children sometimes fret about the many evils to which those they love are exposed. But those endowed with faith can trust the Lord's promise that everything is under control. When upset by frightening events, the faithful can send this message of faith down the neural pathways to their limbic system. Fear is then quieted and replaced with a confidence in God and an appreciation for His watchful care.

In doing so, we can have an experience similar to the one described by Elder Boyd K. Packer:

> A few weeks ago our youngest son and his wife and family stopped to see us. The first one out of the car was our two-year-old grandson. He came running to me with his arms outstretched, shouting, "Gwampa! Gwampa! Gwampa!" He hugged my legs, and I looked down at that smiling face and those big, innocent eyes and thought, "What kind of a world awaits him?" For a moment I had the feeling of anxiety, that fear of the future that so many parents express to us. Everywhere we go fathers and mothers worry about the future of their children in this very troubled world. But then the feeling of assurance came over

me. My fear of the future faded. That guiding, comforting Spirit, with which we in the Church are so familiar, brought to my remembrance what I already knew. The fear of the future was gone. That bright-eyed, little two-year-old can have a good life—a very good life—and so can his children and his grandchildren, even though they will live in a world where there is much of wickedness.[2]

Focus on today rather than fretting about tomorrow

"Take therefore no thought for the morrow: for the morrow shall take thought for the things of itself. Sufficient unto the day is the evil thereof" (Matthew 6:34). This advice was given to disciples who had been called full time to the ministry, and may not apply literally to all of us. For example, we do need to be responsible to support ourselves and our families, and it's important to do what we can to prepare for future eventualities. At the same time, it does no good to worry about what might happen in the future or to be overly cautious or overly concerned. A farmer plants seed in the spring assuming a harvest in the fall. He acts on faith without worrying excessively about drought or other acts of nature that might cause a crop loss. If he focused on all that could go wrong, he might not have the courage to plant at all, which would then obviously guarantee no harvest.

In contradiction to the Lord's advice, some spend a lot of time thinking about all that could go wrong tomorrow. "What if I lose my job?" "What if I get sick?" "What if my child has an accident?" "What if he or she does something really stupid?" Notice that each of these fearful thoughts begins with "What if?" We would generally do ourselves a big favor if we eliminated this question from our mental vocabulary. A better question when some concern comes into our mind might be, "What can I realistically do about it now?" If we ask this question and come up with something practical we can do, it makes sense to do it. If we can't think of anything we can do at the moment, it's best to leave it to the Lord and decide not to dwell on the issue.

The farmer, for example, might be concerned about the possibility of insects destroying his crops. What can he do at the moment? He can pray, and he can make plans to spray his fields. Once done, worrying about it would be of no benefit. Or suppose a parent is concerned about a child getting into trouble. What can the parent practically do about that possibility today? Again, prayer is always a reasonable option. Ensuring consistent home evenings and family scripture study could help. And there may be other ideas that come to mind under inspiration, but at some point, the parent has to trust and let go. Being overly restrictive is not a practical option, and excessive worry would certainly be detrimental.

Turn your cares over to God—quit worrying!

"Humble yourselves therefore under the mighty hand of God, that he may exalt you in due time; Casting all your care upon him; for he careth for you" (1 Peter 5:6–7). "Cast thy burden upon the Lord, and he shall sustain thee: he shall never suffer the righteous to be moved" (Psalm 55:22). Those who tend to worry excessively tend to worry about the future in an unhealthy way, but they also tend to worry about things over which they have no control. In the above and similar scriptures, we are advised to let the Lord deal with those kinds of issues.

Lois is an example of someone who could benefit from this opportunity. Lois tends to worry about everything. Whenever her children are out of her sight, she worries that they may be getting into trouble. She worries about her health. Her mother died at an early age, and Lois frequently thinks that she will too. Lois worries about her husband. She is worried about his weight and his general health. She is also concerned that he isn't as committed to his religion as she wants him to be. She worries about her siblings who still live at home. She is concerned about their exposure to some of the same dysfunctional family dynamics that affected Lois as she was growing up. And on it goes. There is hardly anything that Lois doesn't worry about.

The negative impact of all this worry on Lois is easy to see. She experiences an ongoing high level of stress that is not good for her physically. Given the anxiety caused by her fears, her emotional health suffers as well. Lois also experiences problems interpersonally. Her family resents her fears because it feels to them like a lack of trust. They likewise resent her controlling nature that results from her excessive concerns. Her fears lead her to be overly restrictive with her children, and she is inclined to give frequent warning lectures that irritate both her children and her husband. Beyond that, family and friends are simply annoyed by the constant worry Lois expresses in her general conversation.

Lois could turn 99 percent of her worries over to the Lord. She could do reasonable things to protect her children and teach them correct principles, but then turn the rest over to God. She could quit worrying about her husband's spirituality and let that be between him and the Lord. She could likewise give up worrying about her husband's health, which she can't practically do anything about anyway. Her frequent lectures certainly don't help. She can do reasonable things to improve her own health (reducing worry is probably the most important), but whether she becomes ill or how long she lives can be left in God's hands. The fate of her siblings is also beyond her control, and worry about them can be turned over to the Lord. In short, with sufficient faith, Lois could release herself from most of the worry in her life. The great benefit to Lois and her family if she did so is obvious.

As a side note, it's worth looking at several obstacles that can get in the way as Lois tries to turn worries and burdens over to the Lord. One, Lois has mistakenly combined worry and caring in her mind. She believes that if she quit worrying, that would be equivalent to not caring about those she loves. She has to understand that she can care a great deal about someone but still not worry about them excessively. We know God loves us completely, yet I can't imagine He spends a great deal of time fretting about what we might or might not do. It's hard to imagine a joyous life in heaven if that kind of worry is involved.

As a second problem, Lois operates on the assumption that her worry is protective. As the old saying goes, worry is obviously effective because the things we worry about never happen! Lois is afraid that if she doesn't worry, she won't be prepared if something awful does happen. In effect, she sets herself up to expect the worst so that she will either be emotionally prepared if it happens, or pleasantly relieved if it doesn't. This strategy has a certain logic to it, but it's clearly dysfunctional. It results in people spending a great deal of nervous energy expecting things that are most likely not going to happen. Furthermore, it doesn't help prepare for problems. As suggested below, and in the scriptures quoted earlier (Psalm 55:22), faith in God is the best preparation for any trouble that might come our way.

Lastly, Lois is afraid that if she doesn't worry, she might be held accountable for things that she otherwise might not think to do in preventing problems. In effect, she considers hyper vigilance to be part of what God expects of her. Following the test recommended by Moroni quoted earlier (Moroni 7:13), and based on the result of worry in her life, it's clear that God is not encouraging Lois to think like she does. Rather, God expects Lois to do reasonable things to care for her family and then turn the rest over to Him.

Feed faith, and fear will starve

"Wherefore, be of good cheer, and do not fear, for I the Lord am with you, and will stand by you" (D&C 68:6). "Blessed is the man that trusteth in the Lord, and whose hope the Lord is. For he shall be as a tree planted by the waters, and that spreadeth out her roots by the river, and shall not see when heat cometh, but her leaf shall be green; and shall not be careful in the year of drought, neither shall cease from yielding fruit" (Jeremiah 17:7–8). Faith and fear are opposites that can't both exist at the same time. When faith grows, fear disappears. That is, no doubt, one of the many reasons we are so frequently encouraged by the prophets to do things that build faith.

The formula for building faith is well known to Latter-day Saints. Our understanding is aided by important restoration scriptures such as Alma 32, which defines faith and discusses how to get it to grow within us. The bottom line from all scripture on faith seems to be that building faith is an active process. It involves our doing simple things over time like prayer, gospel study, service to others, keeping the commandments, and so forth. In fact, the simplicity of the process leaves some disappointed. As Elder Neil A. Maxwell has said, "Nevertheless, seekers after the rewards of faith are often disappointed when they are told to study, serve, pray, and worship. As with leprous Naaman, they apparently expect some great thing which requires no obedience to counsel."[3]

In the same address, Elder Maxwell goes on to identify some of the distinct facets of fully formed faith. He suggests that faith in God and in the Lord Jesus Christ includes not only faith in Their existence but also in Their ability to complete Their announced purposes and fulfill Their promises. It includes trust in God's timing, which is often different from ours. And fully developed faith includes trust in God's developmental purposes. By design, life is often difficult for everyone, including the faithful. Faith does not prevent trials, but it does allow those experiencing trouble to face trials confidently, without fear.

Along these lines, Elder M. Russell Ballard has pointed out how faith will eliminate fear for us in our day in the same way that it did for the pioneers of 1847, as they made their way to the Salt Lake Valley:

> Our faith can help us be equally bold and fearless during the course of our respective journeys, whether we are parents working with a troubled child, a single parent trying to raise a worthy family, young people struggling to find a place in a wicked and confusing world, or a single person trying to make the journey through life alone. No matter

how difficult the trail, and regardless of how heavy our load, we can take comfort in knowing that others before us have borne life's most grievous trials and tragedies by looking to heaven for peace, comfort and hopeful assurance. We can know as they knew that God is our Father, that He cares about us individually and collectively, and that as long as we continue to exercise our faith and trust in Him there is nothing to fear in the journey.[4]

Faith as a window through which we view life

The neurological description of the fear response given earlier left out an important feature of the system. There seems to be in the conscious brain a set of schema that help us categorize and interpret the world. The theory is that we are bombarded by so many stimuli that we need an organizational framework in order to make sense of all that goes on in our world. Schemas are that framework. They develop on the basis of our individual experience and then, once learned, constitute a pattern that we impose on ongoing events in order to interpret them and to help make decisions regarding how we will respond.

Each of us may have any number of schema, and they no doubt vary from person to person based on individual experience, but Dr. Louise Gaston, S. Epstein, and others have suggested four that are basic: (1) benevolence versus malevolence of the world; (2) meaningfulness versus meaninglessness of the world; (3) worthiness versus worthlessness of the self; and (4) trustworthiness versus untrustworthiness of others. Where we are with respect to these four basic schema is thought to determine the extent to which we perceive danger in our world. Those who see the world as primarily malevolent and meaningless will naturally respond to events with worry and fear. Likewise, those who view themselves as worthless and others as untrustworthy will characteristically interpret events in a negative way.

Those with faith in the message of scripture have a great advantage with respect to these schema. As suggested next, faith leads to schema that predispose believers to view the world in ways that reduce fear.

Benevolence versus malevolence of the world

Scripture doesn't ignore the reality that this world is a dangerous place, but it helps the faithful realize that they need not fear. "Yea, though I walk through the valley of the shadow of death, I will fear no evil; for thou art with me; thy rod and they staff they comfort me" (Psalm 23:4). Along with this famous quotation from Psalms, the metaphor of faith as a weapon against evil in the world, and as a form of armor, appears several places in scripture. Paul, for example, said:

> Put on the whole armour of God, that ye may be able to stand against the wiles of the devil, . . . Stand therefore, having your loins girt about with truth, and having on the breastplate of righteousness; And your feet shod with the preparation of the gospel of peace; Above all, taking the shield of faith, wherewith ye shall be able to quench all the fiery darts of the wicked. And take the helmet of salvation, and the sword of the Spirit, which is the word of God. (Ephesians 6:11–17)

Our own common experience reinforces the truth in these scriptures. Those with faith have a more optimistic outlook (schema), which results in much less fear when confronting frightening events in the world. A woman kidnapped recently by a gunman who had just killed four people in a jail escape handled the situation with prayer and faith. Over several hours, she ended up getting her attacker to read from faith promoting literature and she bore her testimony to him. The fellow eventually turned himself in and was re-detained without incident.

We attend funerals and marvel at the strength of those of faith who naturally struggle with their loss but have no fear about the future, either for themselves or the departed. We are impressed with those who face debilitating illness or imminent death with courage. All of these people undoubtedly have their moments of concern and times of trial, but they enjoy a protection and a strength because of their faith that results in far less fear and concern than would otherwise be the case. Their faith is as a shield of armor.

Meaningfulness versus meaninglessness of the world

Have you ever wondered how those without faith in God or in an afterlife find meaning in this world? They may find some level of happiness in the moment, and interpersonal relationships have meaning to all of us with or without faith. But those without faith don't have an answer to the basic questions, *Who am I?*, *Why am I here?*, and *Where am I going?* Without an answer to these fundamental questions, there is no way to find anything positive, let alone meaningful, in random acts of violence, health problems, or any other life challenge. Life may be fine as long as everything is going well, but what about when it doesn't? With no sense of

purpose, the inevitable challenges in life are bound to be more disconcert-
ing, and therefore more fear invoking, to those without faith.

Think of the advantage someone has who believes the Lord when He
says:

> And if thou shouldst be cast into the pit, or into the hands of mur-
> derers, and the sentence of death passed upon thee; if thou be cast into
> the deep; if the billowing surge conspire against thee; if fierce winds
> become thine enemy; if the heavens gather blackness, and all the ele-
> ments combine to hedge up the way; and above all, if the very jaws of
> hell shall gape open the mouth wide after thee, know thou, my son,
> that all these things shall give thee experience, and shall be for thy
> good. (D&C 122:7)

There will no doubt be some level of fear experienced even by those
with great faith when facing terrifying circumstances in this life, but that
fear will be mitigated by an understanding that there is an ultimate advantage from the experience. The level of fear will be greatly reduced simply
by understanding the purpose behind the trials that we experience.

The person of faith also benefits greatly when facing one of life's many
inequities. I have a niece who was brain damaged at birth, and over her
thirty years of life was never able to walk, talk, feed herself, or live life in
any normal way. Without the perspective of faith, her life would seem
hopelessly futile. With the perspective of faith, especially truths revealed
during the restoration of the gospel, we know that "all little children are
alive in Christ, and also all they that are without the law. For the power
of redemption cometh on all them that have no law" (Moroni 8:22). My
niece was without the capability of sin and therefore her redemption is
guaranteed. "All things are [hers], whether life or death, or things present, or things to come, all are [hers] and [she is] Christ's, and Christ is
God's" (D&C 76:59). She also has the promise of a perfect resurrection.
Her body will be "restored unto its perfect frame, bone to [her] bone, and
the sinews and the flesh upon them, the spirit and the body to be united
never again to be divided, that they might receive a fulness of joy" (D&C
138:17). My niece's life has ultimate purpose and meaning, but that can
be understood only from the perspective of faith.

Worthiness versus worthlessness of the self

Starting with feeling rejected as a child by her father, Allie developed
a distorted image of herself over the years. By focusing on real or imagined

problems and ignoring positive aspects of herself, Allie came to see herself as damaged goods, unworthy of her place on earth. This was obviously a sad and depressing conclusion about herself, but it also contributed to excessive worry and fear. By seeing herself as worthless and evil, she felt that she needed to be punished. That belief contributed to poor choices and self-destructive behavior. Further, it contributed to a sense of doom as she waited for the next thing to go wrong in her life.

She believed in God, but because she felt so unworthy, that belief did not help relieve her fears. Unfortunately, she had let her experience with her mortal father impact her perception of her Heavenly Father. She thought of God as being also emotionally distant and hard to please. She expected His inevitable wrath, which was a terrifying thought, but she also believed that He would be of no help when problems came up in her life. Interestingly, Allie's conclusion that she deserved to be punished and that God would not help her was reinforced on several occasions when it appeared that her prayers weren't answered. For instance, at one point she prayed long and hard for relief from her depression, but she continued to feel awful in spite of her prayer. That led Allie to conclude that God must not care about her. She believed in the existence of God and that He cared about most people, but it was obvious to Allie that He didn't care about her. In thinking this way, Allie failed to understand several important things about our relationship with God.

First, there is often a timing issue with respect to getting answers to prayer. Allie hoped for and expected immediate relief. She did eventually receive an answer to her prayer, but it didn't come in the time frame she required. As suggested earlier, we need to have the faith to be patient.

Second, and even more important, there are some things that God cannot do. For instance, God cannot overrule our agency and control what we think and do. As long as Allie insisted on thinking negative and depressing thoughts about herself, she felt bad, and those consequences continued until her thinking changed. God could not force Allie to think in a healthy way.

In spite of Allie's conclusion that she didn't matter to God, He obviously does care about her in a fundamental way, as He cares about all of us. "Remember the worth of souls is great in the sight of God; For, behold, the Lord your Redeemer suffered death in the flesh; wherefore he suffered the pain of all men, that all men might repent and come unto him. And he hath risen again from the dead, that he might bring all men unto him, on conditions of repentance, And how great is his joy in the soul that repenteth!" (D&C 18:10–13). Allie needs to understand the fact that Christ suffered for everyone, including her. His love is comprehensive and covers all of us. Allie needs to do her part to make her life work, but she can do that without fear generated by believing that she has been rejected by God. If she changed her basic schema from feeling worthless to realizing her value in the eyes of God, much of the fear in her life would evaporate. She would then also be more motivated to make needed changes in her life.

Trustworthiness versus untrustworthiness

The world is a lot more frightening if we assume that we can't trust ourselves or others. With respect to trusting ourselves, that's much easier to do if we have faith in God. Viewing ourselves as being in partnership with the ultimate power in the universe goes a long way toward building self-confidence. Those with faith also believe that they will not be tested beyond their ability to cope. As Paul said, "There hath no temptation taken you but such as is common to man: but God is faithful, who will not suffer you to be tempted above that ye are able; but will with the temptation also make a way to escape, that ye may be able to bear" (1 Corinthians 10:13; see also Alma 13:28 and D&C 64:20). Faith in this promise will obviously reduce fear when events combine against us and our own resources are insufficient. With faith, we know that circumstances will change or our strength will be increased as necessary to deal with any crisis.

With respect to trusting others, there is always the possibility that someone will disappoint or hurt us. No matter how trustworthy they have been in the past, friends or relatives can surprise us. There are also cases in which trust is destroyed by serious offense. A wife or husband whose spouse has committed adultery, for example, typically agonizes over whether they can ever trust their spouse again. The good news is that with faith in God, faith in one's spouse becomes less important. If emotional security depends on knowing for sure that an offense will not be repeated, that security will be elusive. But if emotional security is founded on faith in God, there is no cause for fear. God, of course, can be trusted implicitly.

The prophet Nephi said, "O Lord, I have trusted in thee, and I will trust in thee forever. I will not put my trust in the arm of flesh; . . . Yea, cursed is he that putteth his trust in man or maketh flesh his arm" (2 Nephi 4:34). We may not ever be able to trust even those close to us completely, but we can be assured of God's support.

Faith that we are on God's side

The discussion so far has focused on how faith in God reduces fear and improves our emotional health. Those who believe in God and know that He is on their side will be less afraid and more self-confident when facing challenges in life. But, according to Joseph Smith, in order for faith to have its maximum benefit in our lives, we must also know that we are on God's side. Joseph Smith pointed this out in *Lectures on Faith*:

> An actual knowledge to any person, that the course of life which he pursues is according to the will of God, is essentially necessary to enable him to have that confidence in God without which no person can obtain eternal life. It was this that enabled the ancient saints to endure all their afflictions and persecution, and to take joyfully the spoiling of their goods, knowing (not believing merely) that they had a more enduring substance.[5]

It takes more than faith in God's existence, or even in His love and mercy. We must also know that our lives are moving in the right direction. This assurance can come by the Spirit as we try to keep the commandments of God. As discussed previously, being worthy of a temple recommend also provides a useful rule of thumb in helping us know that our lives are generally approved of by God. Holding a recommend certainly doesn't mean that we are perfect, but it is an important indicator that we are on the right track. That assurance, coupled with our faith in Jesus Christ, completes our faith and gives us exceptional power in overcoming fear and evil in our lives.

Chapter summary

Fear of God, defined as extreme reverence or awe, is obviously beneficial and necessary. The general emotion of fear, defined as feelings of agitation or anxiety caused by the presence of imminent danger, can be positive or negative, depending on the circumstance and our reaction to the fear. More often than not, it immobilizes us, contributes to sin, and causes significant spiritual, physical, emotional, and interpersonal damage. For that reason, the prophets warn about fear and give a number of suggestions on how it can be managed properly. Following are several questions that we can ask ourselves that indicate whether or not we have this emotion under control:

1. Am I frequently or generally anxious, or do I experience life-altering phobias?
2. Am I afraid of the future or stuck in worry about things that I can't practically do anything about?
3. Do my fears keep me from doing things that I would like to do, or that I know are in my best interest?
4. Do I turn concern about issues beyond my control over to God?
5. Am I constantly building my faith through study, service, prayer, and worship?
6. Do I trust that God will protect me during times of trial?
7. Do I understand that all experience in my life, both positive and negative, will ultimately be to my benefit?
8. Do I understand my worth and value in the eyes of God?
9. Am I dependent on trusting others or do I place my trust in God?

Fear need not wear us down as it typically wears down so many. Thinking in the ways described in scripture can certainly help us avoid this possibility. Anxiety and fear are also among emotional health problems for which a number of very effective techniques have been developed by mental health professionals in recent years. When self-help fails, those resources should not be overlooked.

Furthermore, forgiving ourselves and building self confidence, as discussed in the next chapter, can also help overcome unhealthy fear in our lives.

Notes
1. Gordon B. Hinckley, "God Hath Not Given Us the Spirit of Fear," *Ensign*, Oct. 1984, 2.
2. Boyd K. Packer, "Do Not Fear," *Ensign*, May 2004, 77.
3. Neal A. Maxwell, "Lest Ye Be Wearied and Faint in Your Minds," *Ensign*, May 1991, 88.
4. M. Russell Ballard, "You Have Nothing to Fear from the Journey," *Ensign*, May 1997, 59.
5. Joseph Smith, *Lectures on Faith* (Salt Lake City: Deseret Book, 1985) Lecture 6, Article 2.

8 Building self-esteem

SELF-ESTEEM HAS BECOME AN IMPORTANT issue in educational and mental health circles. It's generally believed that those with a low opinion of their worth are more likely to hurt themselves or others. With low self-confidence, the chances increase that a person will demand attention or go along with the crowd, while the probability of taking initiative in one's life and accomplishing important goals decreases. Those with a healthy self-esteem are more likely to avoid these pitfalls and manage their life in a way that contributes to emotional and mental health.

Almost everyone understands the term *self-esteem* and has a ready definition of what it means. The concept, however, is actually not that straightforward. It's a complicated issue involving a number of elements including cognitive, emotional, and behavioral components. On a cognitive level, self-esteem involves an understanding that we have personal value and are worthy of happiness. On an emotional level, it includes a feeling of well-being and security. Behaviorally, self-esteem involves the ability to confront life productively and to act responsibly in ways that produce acceptance and respect from others. Those with good self-esteem perceive themselves as competent to learn, able to make appropriate decisions, competent in responding to change, and able to handle challenges in life.

Self-esteem is something different from a temporary good feeling created by drugs, a compliment, being in love, or some immediate success. Self-esteem is a lasting way, built over time, of viewing ourselves through positive choices in thought and action. It may wax and wane as new challenges are faced, but there is an underlying confidence that with time, effort, and appropriate action, life can be lived successfully.

As taught in the world, this kind of self-assurance can be developed with or without faith in God; but whether recognized or not, the steps recommended in building self-esteem are based on revealed truth. For instance, experts in the field recommend that self-esteem be built by living honest lives, treating others well, and taking responsibility for our actions. They point out that real self-esteem depends on how we live our lives and how we treat others, not on a series of self-affirmations alone. In other words, we actually have to be a good person, not just tell ourselves that we are. In all these respects, what is needed to build self-esteem amounts to giving our best effort to live the commandments of God.

Perhaps this is why the term *self-esteem* doesn't appear in scripture. Of course, the term itself is of modern origin and wouldn't be expected in ancient texts. But there is little said about the general concept either. For example, I am not aware of any instruction in scripture to have faith in ourselves or to be self-confident—in fact, just the opposite. Likewise, we are not encouraged to love ourselves. For instance, the Apostle Paul cautioned that in the last days men would be "lovers of their own selves, covetous, boasters, proud" (2 Timothy 3:2). Elsewhere, we are admonished to have faith in God, not in ourselves (see 2 Nephi 4:34).

The scriptures make a strong case against narcissism and pride, which in some ways are twisted and perverted versions of self-esteem. As a matter of fact, those who are self-centered and proud generally lack a basic sense of their worth and value and compensate with an exaggerated sense of themselves. Self-esteem involves the self-assurance described above, but in the context of humility. A person with healthy self-esteem will understand *and accept* personal limits and the need to learn from God and others.

In short, self-esteem is a natural by-product of doing the things that are clearly taught in the standard works. The message of scripture includes repeated reminders of the need to live moral lives. There are also a number of references to the intrinsic worth of souls and the infinite and ultimate potential that we all share as literal children of God. As suggested in earlier chapters, there is also much in scripture that supports the idea that imperfections are an inevitable part of the human condition. It does no good to demean ourselves or exaggerate our faults as we undergo the long process of overcoming them. All these factors constitute the foundation of healthy self-esteem.

In addition to an extensive discussion of the fundamental issues related to self-esteem, scripture also provides specific suggestions related, at least indirectly, to developing self-confidence. Several of these are reviewed below.

Practice charity and virtue

"Let thy bowels also be full of charity towards all men, and to the household of faith, and let virtue garnish thy thoughts unceasingly; *then shall thy confidence wax strong* in the presence of God; and the doctrine of the priesthood shall distill upon thy soul as the dews from heaven" (D&C 121:45; emphasis added). Self-confidence or self-esteem results naturally when we practice charity and virtue in thought and action. There are several reasons this happens.

First, having charity and virtue in thought and action is the best way to gain the respect of others. We are naturally attracted to people who we know see the best in us and who have our best interests at heart (those who are charitable). It's also easier to get close to people of integrity because we know where they stand and we have confidence that we can trust them. We may be impressed with those of great intellect or talent, or someone who is strikingly attractive, but we may also be intimidated by such people or put off in some way by them. Others, however, whose strength is in charity and virtue, are not intimidating—which is true even of those who also have great intellect or talent. We feel secure around them and our respect is deep and lasting. If we ourselves are that kind of person, we inevitably have many friends and a stable support group. We know that the people we care about respect us and that they find value in our company. That, in turn, builds our confidence and self-esteem.

Those who practice charity and virtue show respect for others, and they don't cheat, deceive, or steal, which gives those they interact with more reason to trust them. They are naturally on time for appointments (out of respect for others), clean, and supportive. They take responsibility for their actions and don't blame others. They are positive and forgiving. In fact, what's not to like about such a person? When this is true of us, it makes it easy for others to like us, and easy to like ourselves as well. Again, self-esteem thrives in this situation.

In a similar way, it also builds self-confidence to know that our behavior is pleasing to God. As Joseph Smith suggested in *Lectures on Faith* (quoted earlier), we can't have confidence in the presence of God unless we know that our behavior is basically in line with His wishes. We will naturally be uncomfortable around God, or anyone else for that matter, if we have disappointed them in some way. The charity and love we feel from such a person is appreciated, but not that helpful. In a way, it makes it worse to be loved deeply by someone we have disappointed. We naturally react like Mosiah predicted when he said, "They shall quake, and tremble, and shrink beneath the glance of his all-searching eye" (Mosiah 27:31).

Those who are charitable and virtuous in thought and action know that at least that part of their behavior is pleasing to God. Since they also tend to be charitable with themselves, such people are also less likely to let guilt and perfectionism get out of control as described in earlier chapters. They avoid self-criticism and unrighteous self-judgments, which are at the root of many self-esteem problems.

Believe that we are children of God

Self-confidence is greatly increased when we catch a glimpse of our divine heritage and eternal destiny. Moses certainly found this to be true when God appeared to him as described in the first chapter of Moses in the Pearl of Great Price. Moses tells us that God first introduced Himself as the Lord God Almighty and reminded Moses that "there is no God beside me, and all things are present with me, for I know them all" (see Moses 1:6). Moses was also shown the amazing breadth and scope of God's works (see Moses 1:8). Further, Moses was affected physically by being in the presence of God. He fell to the earth when the interview ended, and it was several hours before his strength returned (Moses 1:9–10).

On the surface, it appears that this dramatic introduction was designed to impress Moses with how great God is, but that's something Moses no doubt knew all along. It's more likely that it was intended to set the stage for the revelation to Moses that "thou art my son" (Moses 1:4). Yes, God is almighty, but more important in the narrative, Moses is his son! That makes Moses, and by inference all of us, "heirs of God and joint-heirs with Christ" (Romans 8:17). There could be nothing more significant in defining our eternal worth and potential.

Understanding this truth greatly strengthened Moses' confidence. A little later, now armed with this knowledge, Moses was able to confront Satan directly. Satan came along wanting Moses to worship him, but Moses responded: "Who art thou? For behold, I am a son of God, in the similitude of his Only Begotten; and where is thy glory that I should worship thee?" (Moses 1:13). Our understanding that we too are literal children of God can give us similar strength.

Through his experience with God, Moses also came to understand something quite different: "Now, for this cause I know that man is nothing, which thing I never had supposed" (Moses 1:10). Moses came to also understand his total dependence on God. This understanding may seem to contradict the truth about man's worth and value, but it actually compliments it. The truth is that we can become like God, but not through our own efforts alone. In our mortal state we depend completely on the grace of God to achieve our divine potential. From these two truths, taken together, comes a powerful combination of self-confidence and humility.

Self-confidence through correct choices

As valuable as it is, knowing our divine potential is still sometimes not enough to guarantee a healthy self-esteem. The prophet Enoch probably understood that he was a child of God, but he still lacked self-confidence. When he was first called to be a prophet, Enoch asked God, "Why is it that I have found favor in thy sight, and am but a lad, and all the people hate me; for I am slow of speech; wherefore am I thy servant?" (Moses 6:31). God's response to this question is instructive. As a solution to his lack of confidence, God didn't make a list of Enoch's talents and abilities for him to consider. He didn't say, "Enoch, you're a wonderful person. You have all kinds of abilities. You are this and this and that." Nor did he contradict Enoch's perception that he was hated and slow of speech. Some of us might have been tempted to say, "Oh, Enoch, your speech isn't that bad," or "People don't really hate you." Instead, Enoch was told, "Go forth and do as I have commanded thee, and no man shall pierce thee. Open thy mouth, and it shall be filled, and I will give thee utterance, for all flesh is in my hands, and I will do as seemeth me good" (Moses 6:32).

Enoch was told to confront his fear—to act. God would then bless his efforts and give him whatever he needed to be successful. Actual achievement, not kind and supportive words alone, was necessary in order for Enoch to become self-confident. Enoch had to confront his fear, not just understand his basic worth.

It's not clear if God ever helped Enoch overcome his slow speech directly; but if not, Enoch was clearly blessed in spite of this weakness. People were attracted to him as a speaker (see Moses 6:38), and he spoke with authority and had great success (see Moses 7). It's also clear from the record that it wasn't smooth sailing for Enoch. He had difficulty along the way (see Moses 6:37), and no doubt his share of setbacks. But Enoch's willingness to do the hard work, along with his faithfulness and trust in the Lord, ultimately guaranteed his success. This wouldn't have happened if Enoch had let fear hold him back.

The same thing applies to each of us. We can hope to feel good about ourselves and practice nonstop positive affirmations in our thinking. But if we don't actually put ourselves out there and take risks to serve God and others, our self-confidence won't grow. We need to follow the example of Gordon B. Hinckley when he was a young missionary just beginning his service in England. Of this experience he said: "Those first few weeks, because of illness and opposition which we felt, I was discouraged. I wrote a letter to my good father and said that I felt I was wasting my time and his money. He was my father and stake president, and he was a wise and inspired man. He wrote a very short letter to me which said, 'Dear Gordon, I have your recent letter. I have only one suggestion: forget yourself and go to work.' "[1]

As he went forward and did the right thing, no matter how uncomfortable at the moment, President Hinckley was given strength and his efforts were blessed. Self-esteem grew naturally from the success he eventually experienced and from knowing that his efforts were acceptable to God, even during those times when it looked like nothing was being accomplished.

Not incidentally, this same idea underlies one of the most effective therapeutic techniques when dealing professionally with fears, phobias, and anxiety. As difficult as it is, we are not likely to overcome fear without exposure to what we fear. Those willing to confront their fear directly suffer intense anxiety, and it is very uncomfortable, but that anxiety always subsides with exposure and correct thinking. The person then comes to understand that the monster they have been afraid of all their life has no teeth. Again, this understanding comes only through actual experience, not intellectualization.

The power of the Atonement in building self-esteem

Our self-esteem grows as we put effort into acting responsibly, but the reverse is also true. Self-esteem suffers when we make serious mistakes. Some time ago I attended the rebaptism of a good man who had lost his membership in the Church. It's likely in his case that low self-esteem contributed to his problems in the first place, but it's certain that his self-confidence went to an all-time low as a result of his sin. In fact, he experienced a common cascade effect in which low self-confidence resulted in poor decisions, which further lowered self-confidence, leading to still more mistakes.

To his credit, and with great effort, this individual was eventually able to reverse the process. He eliminated the evil in his life and got back to doing the positive things that connected him with the Spirit. His confidence grew with each correct choice he made, but that alone didn't solve his self-esteem problem. He could feel good about having fought his way back, but that didn't change the reality of how far he had fallen. The memory of his sins and their residual effect in his life caused him great sorrow and led him to feel inferior to others—until, that is, he caught a complete vision of the power of the Atonement in his life.

He came to understand the teachings of Isaiah in a personal way: "[Christ] was wounded for our transgressions, he was bruised for our iniquities: the chastisement of our peace was upon him; and with his stripes we are healed" (Isaiah 53:5). He received a personal testimony that Christ had suffered for *his* sins—all of them, including the most vile. As a result, this individual could forgive himself and move on with all opportunities again open to him. He could go forward with a "perfect brightness of hope" (2 Nephi 31:20), literally healed of the consequences of his sins. He had the same experience as the prophet Alma, who said, "And now, behold, when I thought this, I could remember my pains no more; yea, I was harrowed up by the memory of my sins no more. And oh, what joy, and what marvelous light I did behold; yea, my soul was filled with joy as exceeding as was my pain!" (Alma 36:19–20).

It's interesting to note that some readers misread Alma's comments and assume that the memory of Alma's sins was removed. What Alma actually says is that the *pain* was no longer remembered. Alma still had a memory of his sins, of course, but that memory no longer caused him emotional pain. That's also what happened in the case of the individual described above. After his baptism he stood and bore one of the most powerful testimonies of the Atonement I have ever heard. He was not a person who easily expressed emotion in public, but there he was with wet hair, and tears streaming down his face, as he shared a very personal witness of the Lord's love and mercy. He had literally been healed through the power of the Atonement.

Obstacles to forgiving ourselves

It wasn't easy for this brother to forgive himself. Besides making the considerable effort it took to overcome his weaknesses, he also had to overcome several common assumptions that get in the way of forgiving ourselves. He had to rethink some things in the same way that Courtney did as described below. Courtney made her way back from a history of poor relationships with men and sexual acting out. When I met her, she was an unwed mother with a dark history, but she had changed her life and was back at church. In fact, the changes she had made were dramatic. It was hard to believe that she was the same person who had made the mistakes she had. But in spite of having repented and having formally received the forgiveness of the Church through a disciplinary council, she had trouble forgiving herself. She got hung up on several of the issues listed below.

If I forgive myself, it means I'm not taking my sins seriously

Courtney was qualified to receive the full benefit of the Atonement because of her repentance, including relief from the pain associated with her past sins. It was hard for her to accept this aspect of the Atonement, however, due to a misguided belief that if she let go of the guilt and pain she felt, it would mean that she was minimizing her sins. As a result, she would frequently remind herself of how awful the things she had done were. This naturally led her to also think how awful she must be to have ever participated in such behavior. This kind of thinking inevitably caused guilt and pain, thus subverting the healing she would otherwise have experienced through the Atonement.

There was no need for Courtney to emphasize how awful her sins were or to frequently revisit them in any way. Through her repentance and the Atonement, her sins had been taken away and purged (see 2 Nephi 16:7), blotted out (see Isaiah 43:25), and would not be mentioned by God again (see Ezekiel 18:22). She had been pardoned (see Micah 7:18), and God would not remember her sins and iniquities (see Hebrews 8:12). Courtney should think of her past sins in the same way. There is value in focusing on the Lord's great gift, but no need to review the awful details of her sins.

I need to remember my sins in order to avoid them in the future

The theory behind this assumption is that continued guilt is motivating and will decrease the chances of repeating the offense. As discussed in a previous chapter, guilt can have this effect. But also as discussed previously, guilt works only up to the point of repentance and then only if kept within bounds and not misapplied. Over the long term, love is a better motivator. Courtney will be motivated to keep the commandments in the future because of her love for the Savior and her appreciation of His priceless gift. She will be motivated by her love of correct principles and love of her family, friends, and herself. When motivated in this positive way, Courtney will do the right things because she wants to, not because she is afraid of what might happen if she doesn't. She will avoid thinking in ways that tear at her self-confidence, which will in turn give her greater strength in the struggle ahead.

In essence, relief from pain and guilt will be more motivating to Courtney than keeping them alive in her mind. That's no doubt why the scriptures teach emphatically that sins repented of are pardoned, removed, blotted out, and forgotten. It's as if these sins hadn't happened, which makes it unnecessary to review them or harbor ill will toward ourselves because of them.

It would be very presumptuous to forgive myself

Of course it would be presumptuous, and impossible, to forgive ourselves if that means removing all accountability and all of the consequences of our mistakes. Only Christ has paid the price for our sins, and only He can forgive us in this way. Even after our best effort to repent, we are still not able to unilaterally remove the stain of sin from ourselves, "for we know that it is by grace that we are saved, after all we can do" (2 Nephi 25:23).

At the same time, it is important that we forgive ourselves for the sins we have repented of in the sense of not dwelling on those mistakes and criticizing ourselves for them. This is not only something we *should* do, but something we *must* do. As suggested earlier, the Atonement cannot heal us emotionally if we continue to think in ways that cause us pain. The best healing balm will do little good if we insist on repeatedly ripping the scab off of our wounds.

If I forgive myself, what do I tell others about my past?

Once she had her life on track, Courtney had a natural desire to meet a man worthy to take her to the temple. But what would she tell him about her past? She believed that she would have an obligation to share her sordid history in some detail; but if she did that, he would probably lose respect for her and the relationship might end. This fear naturally made it difficult for her to recognize and take advantage of social opportunities. Actually, in the spirit of the Atonement, it could be argued that Courtney could keep details of her past to herself, even from a future spouse. As suggested above, the Atonement's effect is to remove our sins from the record. It's as if they hadn't happened. In that spirit, there would be no need to share details of her mistakes with anyone before going forward. Why share something that, in effect, hadn't happened?

Of course, Courtney has a son and there are obvious questions that would come up, but those questions could be answered in a general way. "I made some serious mistakes, but I have repented of them and cleared them with the Lord and with my priesthood leaders. I've made a vow to myself not to relive them or to go back there in my mind, and I intend to keep that promise. I need you to judge me based on who I am now, not on the mistakes I made back then." It's likely that a general explanation like this would be sufficient. If not, it would say something about the future husband. Anyone who insists on knowing the details under this circumstance might not be the best marriage candidate.

Courtney's son was young at the time, but she also wondered what she would need to tell him at some point about his father and about the circumstances surrounding his birth. Here again, in the spirit of the Atonement, general information might be sufficient. She could identify the father and the general circumstances of her son's birth, but there would be no need for detail. After all, it's not her history that's relevant to her son, but how much she loves him in the present and how she will treat him in the future. She could also use a discussion on this subject as an opportunity to bear her testimony of the Savior and to reinforce her love for her son. "I have made some mistakes, but thanks to our Savior, those mistakes no longer effect us. But you, son, are no mistake. I love you so much and am so grateful to have you in my life."

Church leaders and self-esteem

The standard works speak indirectly of how to build self-esteem, but modern apostles and prophets have been more direct. President James E. Faust, for example, has said, "It is my firm persuasion that building self-esteem sufficiently to forsake all evil requires a consecration to the saving principles and ordinances of the gospel under divine priesthood authority. It must be consecration to simple, basic Christian principles, including honesty to self and others, forgetting of self, integrity of thought and action. The principles of the restored gospel are so plain, so clear, so compassionate, so endowed with beauty, so graced with love unfeigned, as to be imprinted with the indisputable impress of the Savior himself."[2] This comment supports nicely the idea outlined above that self-esteem grows naturally when we live by the teachings of Christ.

President Hinckley's personal philosophy speaks of a healthy self-regard: "I believe in myself. I do not mean to say this with egotism. But I believe in my capacity and in your capacity to do good, to make some contribution to the society of which we are a part, [and] to grow and develop. . . . I believe in the principle that I can make a difference in this world, be it ever so small."[3] President Hinckley understands his weaknesses and his dependence on God, but he also recognizes his worth and potential to do good. No doubt he would hope for all of us to view ourselves similarly.

Current prophets and apostles speak about the need for self-confidence and self-esteem and how these qualities depend on living gospel principles and serving others. They talk about how our weaknesses can become strengths if we are humble and seek help from the Lord. In this regard, the words of the prophet Ether in the Book of Mormon are often quoted: "And if men come unto me I will show unto them their weaknesses. I give unto men weakness that they may be humble; and my grace is sufficient for all men that humble themselves before me; for if they humble themselves before me, and have faith in me, then will I make weak things become strong unto them" (Ether 12:27). We all have weaknesses, but they become strengths and our self-confidence grows as we put ourselves on the Lord's side and commit to living as He would have us live.

Comments from current apostles and prophets, many quoted in earlier chapters, also talk about the need to avoid unnecessary guilt, to not push ourselves beyond our abilities, to avoid being too critical of ourselves, to take care of ourselves physically, and to focus on the positive in our lives—all of which is important if we are to have self-esteem.

Steps in building self-esteem summarized

1. No matter how you are living your life at the moment, or how you feel about yourself, try to understand your intrinsic worth and value as a child of God.
2. Do your best to practice charity and virtue in how you treat yourself and others. That includes avoiding excessive self-criticism and criticism of others.

3. Focus on and emphasize your strengths, not the things you don't like about yourself.

4. Qualify for a temple recommend.

5. Confront your fears and weaknesses by reaching out to help others. Go out of your way to treat others with kindness, take reasonable risks, and keep your commitments to God and others.

6. Accept the Atonement and forgive yourself after repentance. Don't let guilt get out of control.

7. Eat right, exercise, and get proper rest and recreation.

8. Learn to succeed by pushing yourself to do small things and then greater things.

9. List the things you like about yourself and emphasize items on that list.

10. Identify your weaknesses, and seek help from the Lord to make them into strengths.

11. Get a patriarchal blessing or review the one you have.

12. Forgive others, control your temper, and avoid worry.

13. Don't procrastinate. Move forward diligently with faith in God.

Developing self-confidence is a process that takes time and consistent effort. It won't happen overnight. But those lacking self-esteem must start somewhere. Perhaps by prayerfully considering the items on this list, a place to start will become obvious.

Chapter summary

Self-esteem is an important goal with many benefits. The process of developing self-esteem is fairly straightforward, but certainly not easy. It takes consistency in making good choices and doing our best to live according to correct principles over time. In order to have healthy self-esteem, it's necessary that we be a good person, not simply tell ourselves that we are. Following are some questions that we can ask ourselves that determine the extent of our self-esteem.

1. Do I believe that I have worth and value in the eyes of God and others?

2. Do I focus on the positive aspects of myself?

3. Do I feel that I will be successful in my life if I keep on my current path?

4. Do I treat others and myself charitably?

5. Do I have integrity? Am I honest, unselfish, humble, trustworthy, temperate, and kind?

6. Do I assertively go after things I want in my life, or do I wait for them to come to me?

7. Do I maintain my values when challenged by circumstances or others, or do I go along with the crowd?

8. Do I avoid self-destructive behaviors—things I know will hurt me eventually?

9. Do I feel confident that with the help of God I can handle challenges in my life?

10. Do I have a solid support group of family, friends, and associates?

One of the benefits of self-esteem is that those so blessed are more likely to take initiative in their lives and they are less likely to procrastinate. Procrastination is an interesting phenomenon with multiple causes as discussed in the next chapter.

Notes

1. Gordon B. Hinckley, "Words of the Prophet: Put Your Shoulder to the Wheel," *New Era*, July 2000, 4.

2. James E. Faust, "The Dignity of the Self," *Ensign*, May 1981, 8.

3. "President Hinckley Shares Ten Beliefs with Chamber," *Church News*, 31 Jan. 1998, 4.

9 Perils of procrastination

PROCRASTINATION IS BOTH A CAUSE and effect of emotional and mental health problems. Anger, guilt, fear, and various mental health issues such as depression, anxiety, and low self-esteem can lead to procrastination. In turn, a habit of putting off important assignments and projects creates emotional upset and contributes to depression and other mental health difficulties. This vicious cycle alone makes procrastination a costly problem, not to mention the lost opportunities that procrastination entails, and the fact that putting some things off can have significant eternal implications.

Scripture points out the importance of this life as a "probationary state; a time to prepare to meet God; a time to prepare for that endless state which has been spoken of by us, which is after the resurrection of the dead" (Alma 12:24). Procrastinating repentance during this probationary period can have dire consequences as described by the prophet Samuel in the Book of Mormon: "But behold, your days of probation are past; ye have procrastinated the day of your salvation until it is everlastingly too late, and your destruction is made sure" (Helaman 13:38). Concerned about this inevitable result of procrastinating repentance, the prophet Amulek offered this heartfelt plea: "And now, my brethren, I wish from the inmost part of my heart, yea, with great anxiety even unto pain, that ye would hearken unto my words, and cast off your sins, and not procrastinate the day of your repentance" (Alma 13:27).

Current prophets and apostles are equally direct in their warning about putting off the changes we need to make in our lives. President Spencer

W. Kimball wrote, "One of the most serious human defects in all ages is procrastination."[1] Elder Henry B. Eyring has said, "And so Satan works on both our desire to think we have no cause to repent and our desire to push anything unpleasant into the future. He has tempted you and me, and those we love, with thoughts like this: 'God is so loving; surely He won't hold me personally responsible for mistakes which are simply the result of being human.' And then, if that fails, there is the thought that will almost surely come: 'Well, I may be responsible to repent, but this is not a good time to start. If I wait, later will be better.' "[2]

As Elder Eyring points out, temptation to put off important things is almost universal. Sometimes we procrastinate serious needs such as the need to correct immoral behavior, and other times less critical issues are involved, like putting off home projects or routine self-improvement goals. Who among us has not, at one time or another (and perhaps consistently), put off developing an exercise program, or getting a handle on our diet? Some of us procrastinate paying bills, answering correspondence, or keeping up the yard. We are also likely to put off inviting that great family down the street to go to church with us; or we procrastinate going home teaching or helping a neighbor. For many of us, rationalization and procrastination are finely tuned skills.

Then, too, procrastination often involves more than simply putting off tasks. It can underlie failing to take reasonable risks in life and getting stuck in dead-end situations as a result. Procrastinators may frustrate themselves and others by frequently making big plans but not following through. It may be the root cause when a person is very busy but not very productive; or when someone has such a crowded social calendar that important work doesn't get done. In fact, there is a broad range of symptoms of procrastination.

There is also an equally broad range of basic causes. Some simply choose to put off challenging tasks and concentrate on having fun. Others procrastinate because they are overwhelmed by the pressure of unrealistic expectations, low self-confidence, or some other emotional and mental health issue. Since appropriate steps in overcoming procrastination vary depending on the source of the problem, it's important to sort through the various reasons for one's procrastination when looking for a cure. The same thing that will help a basically lazy person overcome the problem will likely make it worse in the case of someone who procrastinates for emotional reasons. Following are several common causes of procrastination, and remedies appropriate to each cause. But first, a brief description is provided of the common cycle of procrastination.

The cycle of procrastination

As suggested above, most of us procrastinate to some degree, and the symptoms and causes vary in individual cases. But there is a common pattern to procrastination that many of us follow, especially those for whom this is a big problem. The cycle begins with a desire to achieve a particular outcome, which is usually thought of as an imperative: "I've got to get started on that." Then come brief thoughts about the imagined or real advantages of starting the change or project later—"I'll do it later when I don't have this or that problem, or when I'm more likely to be successful." Delays continue and self-criticism begins: "I should have started that earlier." Then we distract ourselves so as not to think of the project or we come up with rationalizations to explain the delay. "I can't concentrate." "I had to go to the party because my best friend depended on me." "I don't have the time." At this stage a person might even pretend to be busy or lie to themselves or others about competing obligations.

Some people can get quite creative at this point. But it doesn't work. It becomes obvious that the desired outcome isn't going to happen, or that a project has to be rushed through with less than desirable results. Now the procrastinator goes back into self-criticism. "There is something wrong with me." "I'm a flake." Self-criticism is again countered by discounting the importance of the desired outcome: "I don't care about that anyway," or by pledging to do better next time, "I'll never do that again." But then, the exact same process is repeated with the next important task.

Part of what seems to perpetuate this cycle is the denial and rationalization used to cover the guilt created by self-criticism. It's difficult to accept responsibility for our choices and learn from our mistakes when we deny reality and rationalize our behavior. Objective observation is much less likely to trigger these kinds of defenses than self-criticism. "That didn't work out the way I had hoped. How can I do it differently next time?" is a much better way to think than, "What a flake I am. When will I ever get it together?" More will be said about how to think in ways that will help us break out of this cycle. These suggestions are given under headings representing various causes of procrastination.

Procrastination due to pleasure seeking

Some people procrastinate primarily because they are self-indulgent and easily frustrated. Those in this group think that the gain associated with long-term goals is not worth the associated pain. They describe the work involved in achieving worthwhile goals as boring, stupid, and painful. They naturally gravitate toward less uncomfortable pursuits and then justify their doing so with irrational thinking such as "I can't stand to be bored," "Doing that is so annoying and useless that I just can't tolerate it," or "I'm a whole lot happier than those sorry people who don't have any fun."

This kind of thinking can lead to nonstop social activity, computer games, television, drugs, alcohol, and so forth as an escape from perceived drudgery. Almost continuous involvement in such activities also provides an escape, at least temporarily, from the guilt and emotional consequences of wasting away a life. Escape from anything unpleasant tends to be reinforcing. Therefore, procrastination, rationalization, and diversions tend to be repeated. The problem is that, in the process, the procrastinator loses respect of self and others, misses the opportunities and fulfillment that come from work and sacrifice, and may jeopardize crucial eternal possibilities. Furthermore, these people likely know at some level that they are ultimately missing out, and it takes effort to keep denying this reality.

Overcoming procrastination in the case of pleasure seekers can be tricky. These people will easily ignore schedules and reminders. Rewards and penalties don't work much better. If a reward/penalty system is self-imposed, these people will simply take the reward without doing the work required and will avoid imposing the penalty for failing to perform. Nor will rewards and punishments from outside do much good. Escape from boredom and drudgery is itself such an engrained reinforcement that other reward/punishment systems usually don't compete.

A basic change in life philosophy is needed. The eat-drink-and-be-merry attitude of pleasure seekers needs to be replaced with one based in reality. The truth is that a go easy, live-for-today attitude won't result in what a person wants out of life. Most of us understand that a complete, happy, and productive life requires some level of sacrifice and effort. Stating this a little differently, the eat-drink-and-be-merry philosophy doesn't work because we don't die tomorrow. We go on living and suffering from the consequences of our poor choices.

Many of our poor choices lead to unhappiness in this life; but if not here, then certainly hereafter. At some point there will inevitably be "a state of awful, fearful looking for the fiery indignation of the wrath of God upon them" (Alma 40:14). Or stated in the positive, "And he that receiveth my Father receiveth my Father's kingdom; therefore all that my Father hath shall be given unto him" (D&C 84:38). Ultimate pleasure seekers are those who take God at His word, who understand the purpose of this life, and who are willing to make the sacrifices and do the hard work necessary to qualify for the blessings promised.

Along with a basic change in philosophy, pleasure seekers need to change their self-talk so that rationalizations are understood for what they are—rational lies. The fact is that the pain in work and sacrifice is largely created by how a person thinks about tasks and responsibilities. Live-for-today procrastinators think of goal-directed effort as hopelessly boring, useless, and awful. No wonder it feels to them hopelessly boring, useless, and awful. But it is possible to redefine hard work and sacrifice. It can be thought of as challenging, not boring. Positives—not negatives—about tasks can become the focus. Hard work can be thought of as a mole hill, not a mountain. Sufficient rest and relaxation can be built in to sustain a productive life.

The self-conning that goes on in the mind of the pleasure seeking procrastinator can also be recognized and changed. For example, the promise to do it later can be recognized as a tool for allowing guilt-free play, not a statement of commitment. Pleasure seekers who think that realistic goals are impossible can realize that they are just giving themselves an excuse for not trying. These people can understand that thinking, "I will do something else now so that I can concentrate on the really important thing later" is simply a ruse to avoid the hard thing. Other examples of rationalizations and how to overcome them will be discussed later, but clearly pleasure seeking procrastinators will need to change their self-talk in order to have any hope of breaking the habit.

I believe all of this to be true, but my guess is that the above statements amount to preaching to the choir. Those taking the trouble to read this book are unlikely to be pleasure seeking procrastinators. You may procrastinate various tasks in an unhealthy way, but not for this reason. On the other hand, you may have children, a spouse, or friends with this problem. In that case, it will be important to remember principles discussed in earlier chapters. There is only so much you can do to help such people. You have a responsibility to live your life productively, but no responsibility to force others to do the same—even those close to you. Encouragement and counsel may be useful in some situations, but lecturing, manipulation, and coercion will do no good. As a matter of fact, a crisis is sometimes the only thing that will get the attention of a pleasure-seeking procrastinator. They can go on with apparent bliss indefinitely until something major occurs that confounds their basic philosophy of life and sends them in a more productive direction.

Procrastinating because of a lack of organization skills

Another cause of procrastination is a simple lack of organizational skills. Sometimes people have so much done for them that they fail to learn how to do for themselves. Or perhaps they grow up in an environment where they don't have the opportunity to learn time management skills. Following are a few suggestions that might help people in this situation.

1. Establish priorities. Not knowing where to begin, or what to work on, can lead to not doing anything at all. Simple prioritizing, such as picking one project to focus on among the many possible, can help. When not overdone, ranking assignments on a daily basis in order of importance is also a good idea. All of this naturally requires taking a little time on a daily basis to organize oneself and to make a daily plan.

2. Break big tasks down into little ones. Instead of trying to do all of a complicated task at once, it helps to break it down into manageable bites. "I can't do all of my home teaching today, but I can do a couple of visits"; or "I don't have time to actually make visits today, but I can call and make appointments for later in the week."

3. Create a time schedule. Rather than being general about it and thinking, "I'll get to that this week," look for and calendar specific times. "I'll work on it Monday and Wednesday afternoons during the kids' nap time."

4. Keep a to-do list. Although a formal system can be helpful, a to-do list need not be a complicated time management and appointment schedule. It can be a simple list of a few items that can be crossed off each day when completed. Simply having a list like this out where it is visible can provide a helpful reminder and motivation to get things done.

5. Set up small rewards for partial achievements. "I'll finish this section of the project and then I'll take a break." "I'll get this done before my favorite television show comes on."

6. Be realistic about what can be done and when. Sometimes we are unrealistic about how much time it will take to do something, and then get discouraged when it takes a lot longer. Other times we think something will take much longer than it actually does. Being as realistic as possible about the time it will take to finish projects is important. It also helps to avoid trying to do something that involves significant concentration while in a chaotic setting. In those cases, it might be worth the extra effort to go to a library or otherwise find a quiet time and place to work.

7. Delegate where possible. Productive people take advantage of the fact that they ordinarily don't have to do important things by themselves. Even things like self-improvement goals are less likely procrastinated if done with a friend. For example, you will be much more likely to follow through on an exercise plan if a friend or friends count on you to join them.

8. Use the ten-minute rule. Establish a rule with yourself that when it's time to do a project, but you don't feel like it, or you don't have the time you thought you would, spend at least ten minutes on it anyway. If it's a motivation problem alone, motivation will normally build if you can just get started. If you don't actually have time for the project, spending ten minutes on it is still better than nothing. In either case, after spending a minimum of ten minutes, a decision can be made about whether or not to continue.

9. Feel good about steps along the way to finishing a project. Rather than thinking about how much more there is to do on a project, focus on what you have already accomplished.

10. Avoid perfectionist expectations. More will be said about this in the next section.

Procrastinating because things have to be done perfectly

Brent is an accomplished carpenter and wood worker. Because of the quality of his work, he is very successful in his business. His wife, on the other hand, is totally frustrated by the fact that he won't take care of projects around the home. Special projects are promised but just don't happen. Even relatively minor repairs and additions to their home never seem to get done. Brent is certainly not lazy. He isn't the pleasure seeking procrastinator described earlier, nor does he lack in time management skills. He is organized, hardworking, and responsible in most areas of his life—except when it comes to projects in his own home.

There are actually two possible explanations for his procrastination, and both may be playing a part. One explanation is a passive-aggressive response to the nagging he gets regularly from his wife. How this problem relates to procrastination will be discussed in the next section. A second, and more likely, explanation lies in the fact that he feels compelled to do home projects perfectly. For instance, Brent hasn't repaired a gouge in the wall because of a web of perfectionist expectations and needs. The hole in the wall is actually in the perfect place for a new home entertainment center he intends to build. The perfect thing would be to get on with the entertainment center rather than spend effort repairing a wall that will just be redone anyway. He hasn't started on the home entertainment center because he hasn't yet found the time or money necessary to proceed. And he hasn't found the time or money needed, primarily because of his elaborate (perfect) plans and the need to do a perfect job using only the best materials. Getting all of that together is a real challenge. The project therefore remains on a perpetual to-do list.

Brent's wife has asked for a sewing center, like the one he did for one of his customers, but he has never gotten around to that either. Again, the time, effort, and money to do the job right—which is the only way he would consider doing it—never seem to be available. And so it is with other projects around the home. Brent and his wife keep waiting for the perfect opportunity to do the perfect job in the perfect way. They have been and will keep waiting for a very long time—unless, that is, Brent changes his perfectionist thinking.

Interestingly, Brent isn't quite so much of a perfectionist at work. There he has no choice but to please his customers, who tend to be more concerned about value than they are about getting a perfect product. At work, he can, therefore, always blame his customers for any less than perfect outcome. At home, however, projects are his total responsibility, and he sees everything he does there as a projection of his ability, values, and worth. He simply won't let himself be represented by a less than perfect product.

Brent is like a lot of people who procrastinate because things have to be done perfectly. For these people, otherwise simple chores become complicated. Such a person may put off cleaning the kitchen because it means scrubbing dishes extensively before putting them in the dishwasher, and then cleaning off all the counters perfectly, and cleaning the floors and the rest of the kitchen before the dishes are done. The same person might not consistently vacuum the carpets because, in addition to running the vacuum over traffic areas, doing the job right also requires moving the furniture, doing baseboards, and so forth. Finding the time and energy to consistently do chores, as they are required to be done by the perfectionist, is a major problem for most people.

Those locked into doing chores or anything else perfectly are therefore much more likely to procrastinate. They also tend to do things in "all or none" fashion. If Brent makes relatively no effort to keep his house in repair, that is somehow easier to justify to himself than making some, but not a perfect, effort. If he began one project, he would feel obligated to do them all at the same time. And each project would need to be done perfectly. Brent is like another person I know who rarely washes or cleans out his car. He hates having a filthy car but finds that easier to justify than doing a less than perfect job keeping it up. Another person has a number of trophies that he enjoys displaying, but when they are displayed, he feels obligated to polish them every week. As a result, they stay in a box in the basement. These folks tend to think, "If I can't do it right, why bother?"

Since procrastination is a symptom of perfectionist thinking in these cases, the underlying perfectionism must be resolved before procrastination can be successfully addressed. Please refer back to chapters 2 and 3, which discuss a number of issues related to perfectionism and how this problem can be overcome.

Procrastinating because of anger

Sometimes we avoid or put off effort to achieve a desirable goal out of spite. For instance, an otherwise faithful member of the Church decides, "I'm not going to pay tithing as long as that man is bishop." Or a student who wants to get good grades for his own reasons may put off studying, thinking, "Why work hard to get good grades? My parents just yell at me anyway." Then there is the lady who promised herself that she would work on her diet. While out to lunch, her husband made a comment about her diet as she was about to order. In response, she said to the waiter, "Make that a *double* order of fries." In situations like these, people put off what they would otherwise do simply because they don't want to give someone who has offended them the satisfaction of addressing their complaint.

It's easy, but foolish, in these instances to blame the object of our anger for the delay. Putting off her diet plans and consuming those French fries was, in her mind, her husband's fault. She tells herself, "He makes me so mad. I won't let him get away with his constant nagging." Granted, the husband should have kept his opinion to himself and respected his wife's right to manage her own life, but his problem does not control her choices. The wife must recognize her anger for what it is and admit responsibility for her actions or she will continue to have difficulty reaching her goal. Whenever we procrastinate self-improvement efforts or resort to self-destructive behavior in anger, we have no one to blame but ourselves.

As in the preceding examples, anger can result in procrastination when we act out of spite. Anger can also affect motivation to do important things in a more subtle or general way. For example, a husband and wife who have been arguing may put off couple prayer or cancel their plans to go out together. In the process, they miss important opportunities to resolve their anger. Anger at oneself may lower self-confidence to the point that a person gives up on important goals or avoids issues that become too painful. Someone else might act in a passive aggressive way in an attempt to indirectly control an irritating situation. This was probably an issue in the case of Brent, outlined earlier. He was frequently angry about his wife's complaints that he didn't do anything around the house. Rather than confront her directly, which usually didn't work since her position was hard to argue against, he let his anger affect decisions about projects for his wife. Dragging his feet was a way of making a statement without having to do it directly.

As in the case of perfectionists, those who procrastinate because of anger must resolve that issue before they will be successful in confronting their procrastination. Several suggestions regarding anger management can be found in chapter 6.

Procrastination due to a fear of success or fear of failure

It's sometimes hard to understand how anyone could be afraid of success, but it does happen. With success often comes expectations, public notice, or requirements to act responsibly in some additional way. Any of these prospects can be so frightening that a person will procrastinate the steps to be successful. "If I get good grades this semester, I won't have an excuse. I'll have to get good grades every semester." "If I do a great job, I'll get promoted. But I'm afraid that I would fail as a manager." Not achieving in these cases is better than facing the uncertainties and fears associated with success.

Others worry that their success will be intimidating to others and therefore put a crimp in their social life. I lived in Polynesia for a few years, and there seemed to be a general attitude among young people there that getting good grades just wasn't cool. Students dedicated to their studies risked losing friends and being perceived as arrogant snobs. Procrastinating homework was fairly common in that environment.

Another fear-based cause of procrastination is the fear of failing. On the surface, this can also be hard to understand. Since procrastination is a good way to guarantee failure, it would seem like fear of failure would reduce the tendency to put things off. The fact is that, for some people, failing because of not trying is less painful than trying and then failing. Perhaps this is because these people are afraid to discover how capable they really are. (Or perhaps they are afraid that others will discover any inadequacies.) Even if they fail at something, these people can maintain at least an illusion of competence since they never truly commit themselves. "I would have been successful if I had put effort into it, but it just wasn't that important to me."

Fear of failure is also a reason some people do things at the last minute. Again, there is a built-in excuse for failure. "It would have worked if I had started earlier. I did amazingly well under the circumstances." The fact that the impossible circumstance was created by a choice to procrastinate typically goes unrecognized. In effect, the individual finds comfort in having an excuse for failure, even if that excuse results from his or her own inadequacy.

Worriers recognize that things aren't right in their lives, but they are afraid to make changes because of a fear that things will be made worse— whether they fail or succeed—or they are so worried about outcomes that they build in excuses in case of failure. Those who procrastinate for these reasons must address their worry before they will have much success conquering procrastination. The reader is referred back to chapter 7 for a discussion of overcoming worry and fear in our life.

Other reasons for procrastination

The primary reasons for procrastination have been referred to above; but to be complete, there are other possibilities. For instance, some procrastinate because they are dreamers. Dreamers have great, or perhaps grandiose, ideas, but they hate the details. Success with projects is in the details, which means that dreamers will go from one idea to another, putting off the detail work necessary for success. Overachievers procrastinate primarily because they have too much on their plate. These are typically either people who need to learn to say no to some requests, or those with overly high expectations for themselves. They may or may not be perfectionists, but they feel obligated to do every good thing that comes along. Procrastination then becomes inevitable since it's virtually impossible to do everything that overachievers believe is necessary.

Lastly, some people procrastinate because they believe that they function best under pressure. They believe, erroneously, that they are more creative, more efficient, and more productive when they wait until the last minute to begin projects. The challenge of getting the job done under that circumstance is fulfilling and adds excitement to projects. But, unfortunately, when done at the last minute, the quality of work is inevitably lower and the probability of success reduced.

People who procrastinate for any of these reasons will need to check their self-talk and get a handle on irrational thought. They must learn to recognize and confront their rationalizations as described in the next two sections.

Rebutting rationalizations that keep us from completing important projects

Rationalizations lose their effectiveness when they are recognized for what they are and when counter logic is used against them. A number of years ago, two psychologists, Albert Ellis and William Knaus, reviewed several common rationalizations that support procrastinating important projects. Their ideas, intermixed with some of my own, may be of value.

1. I work best under pressure, so I will put off this task until the pressure is on. Ability to complete tasks may seem to be enhanced under time pressure, but that is likely to be more illusion than reality. Concentration may be heightened by time constraints, and it's easier to say no to distractions; but these advantages won't compensate for the disadvantages of last-minute effort. Such effort often involves late hours, disruption in lifestyle, and frustration in not being able to gather materials or information effectively. Simply put, projects cannot be done as well, or completed as efficiently, when done at the last minute.

2. I don't know how to get started or how to do the job properly. Some amount of pre-planning when contemplating a project is useful, but that can easily be overdone. In fact, there is a descriptive term that applies when pre-planning is overdone: "paralysis by analysis." Normally a person is at a loss even to know the right questions to ask about a task until after some experience with it. Effective learning requires picking a starting point—any starting point is better than none—and beginning. Then questions can be asked and help solicited along the way.

3. I don't really want to do it. Once a decision has been made that completing an assignment will pay long-term dividends and that it should be done, not wanting to do it is irrelevant. All this means is that you had better start the job and get it over with as soon as possible. At least then it will be out of the way. In addition, it's important to remember that even an unpleasant task can become a "want to" if the long-term advantages are emphasized. It's all in how we think about it.

4. It really doesn't matter if I get it done or not. It's true that we have our agency and no task *must* be completed. At the same time, it's also true that "there is a law, irrevocably decreed in heaven before the foundations of this world, upon which all blessings are predicated—And when we obtain any blessing from God, it is by obedience to that law upon which it is predicated" (D&C 130:20–21). No matter what we say to ourselves, it always matters if we put off doing things upon which important blessings depend.

5. It will be easier if I am in the mood, so I'll wait until I feel more ready for it. The problem in waiting for the right mood is that it may never come. Motivation for completing assignments and interest in them generally depend on becoming involved. It's also true that most things become enjoyable once we start. You may be like me. Any number of times I have not felt like doing something only to find that it was quite enjoyable once I got into it.

6. Waiting until the last minute saves a lot of time and energy. Time may be saved by doing a job poorly, but there is no reason that a good effort should take more time at one point than at another. As a matter of fact, early effort often takes less time and energy because of factors such as easier access to information, avoiding long lines, and working in conjunction with other tasks.

7. I could have done it sooner, but circumstances beyond my control prevented it. Circumstances do interfere with plans; and as suggested in chapter 2, it's unhealthy to feel guilty about things over which we have no control. On the other hand, it's unhealthy to excuse ourselves for the results of overt procrastination. Obviously, one of the reasons to complete assignments early is to allow for circumstances that come up unexpectedly.

8. If I do this now, I will never again have the chance to do what I would rather do right now. "I'm on a roll with this computer game. I can't stop now." "John is only in town this weekend; I have to spend time with him." The truth is that chronic procrastinators typically don't plan very well. With a reasonable schedule and ordinary planning ability, situations rarely come up that represent a genuine once-in-a-lifetime opportunity. The game can always be interrupted; and normally, plans can be made that allow both time for important projects and time with a friend in town for the weekend.

9. I have worked on this so long that I don't want to do it anymore. This rationale, when used by a procrastinator, usually means that the job has been going on too long because various aspects of it keep being put off. Without procrastination and under normal circumstances, the desire to complete a project increases the closer to its completion. This is especially true if the task is an unpleasant one.

Whether these or other rationalizations are involved, procrastinators need to listen to how they think and confront the "rational lies" they tell themselves.

Common rationalizations for procrastinating repentance

Listening for rationalizations and confronting them is particularly important when the issue we are putting off has eternal implications. As suggested earlier, the Lord has clearly warned about the danger of procrastinating repentance. Following is a brief discussion of several common rationalizations that contribute to this problem.

1. It will hurt others if I repent. "By this ye may know if a man repenteth of his sins— behold, he will confess them and forsake them" (D&C 58:43). I know of several cases in which individuals have procrastinated completing the repentance process because they have convinced themselves that confessing and resolving sin would harm those they love. For example, a bishop let a counseling situation get out of control and ended up committing adultery. This problem obviously needed to be confronted and confessed. But he put it off and continued to serve as bishop, attend the temple, and generally serve unworthily. His thinking was, "My wife and kids are innocent in all of this. If I come forward, it will cause them immense pain, and I can't do that to them." He also thought about the impact his behavior would have on ward and stake members once they discovered his sin.

This bishop understood the doctrine and knew the truth, but he convinced himself that he was willing to pay the price for his deception. He even went so far as to consider his actions to be noble in a way. The reality of his sin and his hypocritical response was tearing him apart, but he considered that to be part of the price he had to pay. Of course, this bishop should have done things the Lord's way, which involves *both* forsaking and confessing serious sin. In this case, the sin came to light before the bishop got around to confessing, and the results for his family and his ward were even more devastating than they would have been if he had repented properly and quickly.

2. There is plenty of time to repent later. The Lord himself clearly taught the fallacy in this rationalization in the parable of the wise and foolish virgins (see Matthew 25:1–13). The five foolish virgins could not make up for their lack of preparation at the last minute. These women came to the Lord, pleading that they be allowed in to the marriage feast, but the bridegroom said, "I know you not" (v. 12) and did not allow them to enter. This parable is directed primarily to those of us who know the Savior and expect His coming. The Lord tells us that we must "watch therefore, for ye know neither the day nor the hour wherein the Son of man cometh" (v. 13). We cannot prepare at the last minute.

The same message was also taught in the parable of the evil servant who thought that his employer would be delayed (Matthew 24:44–51). The evil servant therefore began "to smite his fellowservants, and to eat and drink with the drunken" (v. 49). But "the lord of that servant shall come in a day when he looketh not for him, and in an hour that he is not aware of. And shall cut him asunder, and appoint him his portion with the hypocrites: there shall be weeping and gnashing of teeth" (vv. 50–51).

Speaking to the same theme, the prophet Amulek in the Book of Mormon taught that "this life is the time for men to prepare to meet God; yea, behold the day of this life is the day for men to perform their labors. And now, as I said unto you before, as ye have had so many witnesses, therefore, I beseech of you that ye do not procrastinate the day of your repentance until the end; for after this day of life, which is given us to prepare for eternity, behold, if we do not improve our time while in this life, then cometh the night of darkness wherein there can be no labor performed" (Alma 34:32–33).

Bottom line: there is no benefit in delaying repentance, but many good reasons to get on with it. As the scriptures make clear, those who procrastinate repentance may end up everlastingly too late. It's also true that putting off repentance makes it harder. The longer we sin, the stronger unhealthy habits become. In addition, faith, which is so important in successful repentance, is weakened. Finally, there are lost opportunities the longer we wait.

We may ultimately be forgiven, but we will have missed a number of important benefits that we would otherwise have enjoyed.

3. I can't do it. It's too hard. Some changes, such as overcoming addictions to drugs, pornography, and so forth, can be extremely difficult, but never impossible. One of the most quoted scriptures in the Book of Mormon emphasizes this truth: "And it came to pass that I, Nephi, said unto my father: I will go and do the things which the Lord hath commanded, for I know that the Lord giveth no commandments unto the children of men, save he shall prepare a way for them that they may accomplish the thing which he commandeth them" (1 Nephi 3:7).

We also have the promise in scripture, referenced in an earlier chapter, that we will not be tempted beyond our ability to withstand. This same promise appears throughout the standard works (see Psalm 37:23; 1 Corinthians 10:13; 1 Nephi 3:7; D&C 95:1). However difficult some changes are, and no matter the number of relapses along the way, it is always possible to repent given sufficient faith and resolve.

4. My sins are not that big a deal when compared to others. I have no need to repent. Probably the classic refutation to this common rationalization is given by Nephi in the Book of Mormon. Part of his words were quoted earlier, but they are also relevant here.

> Yea, and there shall be many which shall say: Eat, drink, and be merry, for tomorrow we die; and it shall be well with us. And there shall also be many which shall say: Eat, drink, and be merry; nevertheless, fear God—he will justify in committing a little sin; yea, lie a little, take the advantage of one because of his words, dig a pit for thy neighbor; there is no harm in this; and do all these things, for tomorrow we die; and if it so be that we are guilty, God will beat us with a few stripes, and at last we shall be saved in the kingdom of God. Yea, and there shall be many which shall teach after this manner, false and vain and foolish doctrines, and shall be puffed up in their hearts, and shall seek deep to hide their counsels from the Lord; and their works shall be in the dark. (2 Nephi 28:7–9)

The problem with sin, even when talking about less consequential mistakes, is that "no unclean thing can dwell with God." Actually the entire quote from the prophet Nephi is, "Wherefore, if ye have sought to do wickedly in the days of your probation, then ye are found unclean before the judgment-seat of God; and no unclean thing can dwell with God; wherefore, ye must be cast off forever" (1 Nephi 10:21). The same point is made even more directly by the Lord in the Doctrine and Covenants: "For I the Lord cannot look upon sin with the least degree of allowance" (1:31).

God will not tolerate sin in any degree not because He is intolerant, but because the celestial world in which He dwells would cease to be celestial if people resided there who were not completely dependable. This is the sad truth for those who procrastinate their repentance. The good news comes in the next verse to the one just quoted: "Nevertheless, he that repents and does the commandments of the Lord shall be forgiven" (D&C 1:32).

Chapter summary

Procrastination in any of its forms is very costly, especially when what is put off affects the eternities. Those with a significant problem in this area will inevitably experience lost opportunity as well as emotional and mental health complications until they overcome the habit. Following are a few questions that reveal a procrastination problem.

1. Do others frequently complain about my being late or that I fail to follow through on promises?
2. Are there a number of projects that I either never seem to finish or never start in the first place?
3. Do I honestly qualify for a temple recommend?
4. Is there a self-improvement goal that I would very much like to accomplish but keep putting off?
5. Do I organize my time on a daily basis in at least a rudimentary way?
6. Do those whose opinions I respect see me as a dependable and accomplished person?

All of us are tempted to put off some important things at times, and many of the issues discussed in previous chapters impact this tendency. For example, perfectionism, anger, guilt, worry, and low self-esteem all play a part. Depending on the particular cause of procrastination, issues discussed in the previous chapters are relevant in overcoming the problem. The next and concluding chapter includes a review of these principles.

Notes
1. Spencer W. Kimball, *The Teachings of Spencer W. Kimball*, edited by Edward L. Kimball (Salt Lake City: Bookcraft, 1982), 48.
2. Henry B. Eyring, "Do Not Delay," *Ensign*, Nov. 1999, 33.

10 Applying remedies for emotional headaches

EMOTIONAL AND MENTAL HEALTH ISSUES certainly cause turbulence in our ride through life. But God has not left us alone to deal with these problems. As described in previous chapters, any number of antidotes to emotional headaches can be found in scripture. And as you have probably noticed, these remedies have multiple effects. A virtue that will help us improve our self-esteem also helps us overcome procrastination. Limiting guilt to its positive expression will help us manage anger and worry, and it will also improve self-confidence. Forgiveness and faith are general principles that benefit our emotional lives in a number of ways. As a result of these multiple effects, when we follow the Lord's counsel and solve emotional problems in one area, we will probably see a benefit in other areas as well.

And happily, the remedies available in scripture are of the over-the-counter variety, and no charge is involved. But these remedies are not really free. Effort is obviously required to think and act in the ways recommended by the Lord. But effort directed by the Lord is much preferable to struggling with emotional headaches on our own. As the Lord said, "Take my yoke upon you, and learn of me; for I am meek and lowly in heart: and ye shall find rest to your souls. For my yoke is easy, and my burden is light" (Matthew 11:29–30). Oftentimes a cure to an emotional headache, such as forgiveness, will even seem to be impossible. "I can never forgive him for what he has done to me." But one can forgive. And doing so will be easier, by far, than carrying an emotional burden of hate.

The difficulty, however, in applying some of these antidotes, like forgiveness for example, does suggest the value in getting help in some cases. Help in the process is particularly important in the case of serious emotional upset or mental health problems. This help can come from several sources: God, priesthood leaders, friends and family, professional counseling, and medication. Since all of these can be important, each will be discussed briefly below.

Help in overcoming emotional problems

Seeking God's help when overcoming emotional problems is important in two respects. First, the Spirit can direct us regarding where to spend self-improvement energy most wisely. As King Benjamin pointed out in the Book of Mormon, it's important to be balanced in our efforts, and there is an order required in effective self-improvement. "And see that all these things are done in wisdom and order; for it is not requisite that a man should run faster than he has strength. And again, it is expedient that he should be diligent, that thereby he might win the prize; therefore, all things must be done in order" (Mosiah 4:27). The Spirit can help us find that balance and help us prioritize our efforts. King Benjamin also points to the fact that we need to be diligent. This is true since most spiritual and emotional growth occurs gradually over time. Overnight success is rare, but continued effort will win the prize. When this blessing is sought, the Comforter can help us find the required patience.

Second, divine support is always helpful, and sometimes critical, in finding solutions to emotional problems. Even those outside the gospel understand this point. For instance, virtually all effective programs treating various addictive behaviors have a religious element that involves reaching beyond ourselves and accessing a higher power. Also, certain remedies such as faith and forgiveness often come to us in part as a gift from God. For example, many trying to forgive serious offenses report that their burden seemed to be lifted by God—very much as a gift—after they had done all that they could do on their own.

While spiritual direction and support is critical in overcoming emotional problems, in fairness, it should be pointed out that the process through which we receive this help can sometimes be confusing. As described earlier, emotions are affected by physiological processes, our thoughts, and outside influences. At times it can be a challenge to distinguish between our own thoughts and the attendant emotion generated, and thoughts brought to us by the Spirit. It's sometimes difficult even for those seasoned by experience with the Spirit to sort out the difference, let alone those inexperienced in such matters. There are also a few who are overly influenced by what a friend of mine has referred to as the "goose bump gospel." As the thinking goes, if we feel emotion, and especially if that emotion brings us to tears, then we must be feeling the Spirit. Or conversely, if we have no such emotional experience, we are apparently on our own. President Howard W. Hunter's observation should help with any confusion in this regard:

> I get concerned when it appears that strong emotion or free-flowing tears are equated with the presence of the Spirit. Certainly the Spirit of the Lord can bring strong emotional feelings, including tears, but that outward manifestation ought not to be confused with the presence of the Spirit itself. I have watched a great many of my brethren over the years and we have shared some rare and unspeakable spiritual experiences together. Those experiences have all been different, each special in its own way, and such sacred moments may or may not be accompanied by tears. Very often they are, but sometimes they are accompanied by total silence. Other times they are accompanied by joy. Always they are accompanied by a great manifestation of the truth, of revelation to the heart. . . . Listen for the truth, hearken to the doctrine and let the manifestation of the spirit come as it may in all of its many and varied forms. Stay with solid principles; teach from a pure heart. Then the Spirit will penetrate your mind and heart and every mind and heart of your students.[1]

As President Hunter suggests, part of the secret in ensuring that we are feeling the Spirit, as opposed to other influences, seems to involve sticking with solid principles. The truth registers with us and conforms to other truths that we already know. It works for us and for others and moves us toward Christ and His gospel (see Moroni 7:12). Counterfeit influences, or those generated by our own minds, may feel the same at times, but send us ultimately contrary to solid principles. Following these impressions may cause momentary relief, but locks us up over the longer term.

When we are confused about this issue, counsel from priesthood leaders might also help in sorting out whether the emotion we have felt is from God or some other source. In fact, the support and guidance of priesthood leaders can be generally helpful as we struggle with emotional issues. Their advice and blessing may be just what we need at times. Speaking of priesthood blessings, however, there may be cases in which these blessings do not result in the relief we seek. In those instances, we should not automatically assume a lack of faith, or a failure of the blessing. Sometimes our "thorns in the flesh" are not removed for reasons known only to the Lord (see 2 Corinthians 12:7–9). At other times, the Lord would certainly bless

us with relief from our emotional or mental health issues if He could, but
He can't. As suggested earlier, God cannot override our agency to think as
we choose. If we insist on thinking in ways that cause emotional or mental
health problems, God will not be able to remove the natural consequences
of our destructive thinking.

Whether a priesthood leader, friend, or family member, it always helps
to have the support of those who love us on our side as we face emotional
problems—support that is, not necessarily their advice and certainly not
their criticism. Sometimes friends or family members feel obligated to give
advice when what is needed is simply someone who cares. Other times, in
the process of thinking that they are helping, others actually make things
worse by being critical. Among any number of examples that could be
given, people have been criticized for being lazy when their procrastination was actually due to caring too much about being perfect. People have
been criticized for experiencing symptoms of depression when, in fact, the
depressed person has been fighting the disease with all of his or her might.
People have been ridiculed for their fears in the misguided attempt to get
them to see the irrationality of their concerns.

As we open up our emotional issues to others, we must be prepared to
filter the resulting "help" we get. At times it will be just what's needed. At
other times, we will need to let advice or comments go in one ear and out
the other. When the shoe is on the other foot and someone we love is hurting, it helps to remember certain gospel principles. Rather than assume
that we know the answer to their problem, we need to be humble. We need
to limit advice and simply love and have faith in the person who is struggling. We need to follow the advice given by the prophet Alma in the Book
of Mormon when he suggested that we "bear one another's burdens, that
they may be light; Yea, and [be] willing to mourn with those that mourn;
yea, and comfort those that stand in need of comfort" (Mosiah 18:8–9).

Finally, a few words are needed regarding the value of professional
counseling and medication when we struggle with emotional and mental
health issues. After more than thirty years in the mental health field, I
have learned that (1) many people experiencing mental and emotional
health problems can be helped by an experienced counselor; and (2) there
are many incompetent counselors in practice who, at best, won't be of
much help; and at worst, will do damage. If you or someone you love
seeks professional counseling, make sure that you audit the process. First
of all, rather than disparage your values, the therapist should work within
them, and he or she should not encourage you to do things that contradict

what you know to be true from scripture and other trusted sources. Also, after no more than a few visits, you should have a degree of faith in the counselor, and it should be obvious that his or her intervention is helping. If that is not the case, find someone else.

Over the years, I have also learned that there are many competent therapists available and that their interventions can be lifesaving. As a matter of fact, some problems are not likely to be resolved without professional help, and most emotional problems are more easily tackled with this kind of help. After all, if you were trying to learn any new and particularly difficult skill, you would seek out a coach or teacher if possible. That would likely be true if you wanted to learn to play the piano or play golf. People hire tax consultants and go to cooking schools. Why not seek an experienced coach if you are trying to improve your skills in anger management or some other emotional issue? You may be able to do it on your own; but why do it the hard way if you don't have to?

Regarding medications, I have seen them do wonders in some cases. Some Latter-day Saints and others believe that psychotropic medications have horrible side effects and should be avoided. Even when they work, some people believe these medications to be a crutch and therefore a sign of weakness on the part of those who use them. Interestingly, these same people probably wouldn't have a problem with someone taking diuretics or beta blockers to lower blood pressure, or insulin to counter the effects of diabetes.

In my opinion, a trial on psychotropic medication is a good idea for those suffering from serious emotional or mental health issues and for whom talk therapy has so far not helped. If there are negative side effects from the medication, then the prescription and dosages can be adjusted. If these medications don't help, they can be discontinued. But if they make a difference, as I believe will become more often the case with increased medical understanding, the results can be lifesaving.

Remedies for emotional headaches summarized

Since they are all important, each of the principles discussed earlier is summarized below. Page numbers are given where a discussion of the principle begins in this book; but more important, a scriptural reference or two is also provided. Keep in mind that the principle may be discussed in more than one place in various chapters and that other scriptural references exist for most principles cited. The citations given are to be considered basically as a starting point for further investigation.

When summarized as they are here, the principles listed can provide a basic inventory of your emotional health. You might wish to review the principles in terms of how well you apply them in your life. If you notice problem areas, that is obviously a place to invest self-improvement energy, and you might wish to review the relevant section of this book for pointers on how to proceed. But don't try too hard. Those who have stuck with me this far are likely to be highly motivated, driven people. If you err, it will probably be that you end up trying too hard to improve. For example, in my experience, perfectionists often frustrate themselves by becoming perfectionists about not being a perfectionist!

If you do establish goals to improve your emotional health, the words of Elder Neal A. Maxwell are insightful regarding the basic attitude to have during the process. He urged us to "distinguish more clearly between divine discontent and the devil's dissonance, between dissatisfaction with self and disdain for self. We need the first and must shun the second, remembering that when conscience calls to us from the next ridge, it is not solely to scold but also to beckon."[2] In the same talk, Elder Maxwell also pointed out that we all tend to be "dishonest bookkeepers and need confirming 'outside auditors.' " As you take the time to review your status with respect to the principles summarized here, the Spirit needs to be invited along in order to audit your conclusions.

Principles

- Problems are a lot more painful and difficult to bear if we fail to remember that they are always temporary (pp. x and xii; D&C 121:7).

- The pain of the moment is easier to bear and has meaning when we see its connection to our ultimate goal, and when we focus on promised blessings (pp. x and xii; D&C 121:8).

- Even when facing something awful, not everything in our life is bad. Focusing on what's right can help us deal with the negative (p. x; D&C 121:9–10).

- Guilt is a useful emotion when used properly, but it can be taken too far (p. 1; Alma 15:3; Russell M. Nelson, "Perfection Pending," Ensign, Nov. 1995, 86).

- Guilt is unnecessary and harmful if continued after we have repented (p. 3; Alma 36:19–20; Isaiah 1:18).

- It's unnecessary and harmful to feel guilty about things we can't control (p. 7; Revelation 12:4).

- It's unnecessary and harmful to feel guilty about essentially normal behavior (p. 10; Russell M. Nelson, "Perfection Pending," *Ensign*, Nov. 1995, 86).

- It's unnecessary and harmful to feel guilty about nonmoral issues (p. 11; John 9:1–3; 2 Corinthians 12:7–9).

- It's a mistake to think that we must be perfect in this life (p. 18; Mosiah 4:27; D&C 67:13–14).

- It's a mistake to think that we must be perfect in everything (p. 20; D&C 138:9).

- Mistakes and perfection are not contradictory concepts (p. 22; 2 Nephi 2:22–25; Ether 12:27–28; D&C 38:14).

- We don't depend on ourselves to become perfect. We become perfect only in Christ (p. 23; Moroni 10:32–33).

- In order to improve and progress, it's *not* necessary to put extreme pressure on ourselves (p. 23; 1 Corinthians 13:1–3; Neal A. Maxwell, "Notwithstanding My Weakness," *Ensign*, Nov. 1976, 23).

- As an adult, it's sometimes useful to play before our work is done (p. 27; JST, Matthew 4:1).

- Since we don't have the perfect understanding and knowledge that God does, it's best not to swear to the truth of things, or to be rigid and black and white in our conclusions (p. 29; 3 Nephi 12:33–37).

- It helps to think of projects and tasks in terms of "want to," not "have to" (p. 34; John A. Widtsoe, *Discourses of Brigham Young* [Salt Lake City: Deseret Book 1954], 62).

- It's inappropriate and harmful to think about aspects of ourselves or others in terms of "never" and "always" (p. 37; Matthew 20:1–16).

- We need to avoid jumping to general conclusions on the basis of one, or just a few, instances of something (p. 38; John 7:24).

- Since the focus of our thoughts largely determines our feelings and the choices we make, it's important to dwell on the positive rather than the negative (p. 47; 3 Nephi 13:43–44).

- We need to look for things that are positive and praiseworthy in ourselves and others (p. 49; Articles of Faith 1:13).

- Being overly analytical or looking at things too closely can be a mistake (p. 49; Gordon B. Hinckley, address delivered 18 June 1983 at BYU—Hawaii).

- We are to press forward doing the best we can even if the path ahead is not altogether clear (p. 52; Neal A Maxwell, "Apply the Atoning Blood of Christ," *Ensign*, Nov., 1997, 22).

- Positive thinking needs to be balanced with a concern about planning, preparation, and avoiding sin (p. 53; D&C 63:58).

- We need to forgive others of their offenses against us no matter how often repeated, whether major or minor, and whether or not a person apologizes (p. 56; D&C 64:8–10).

- Forgiveness means that we no longer harbor ill will or suffer emotionally from an offense. It doesn't mean that we forget (p. 59; Genesis 50:21).

- We don't have to tolerate what people do just because we forgive them for doing it (p. 61).

- Forgiving someone does not mean that we excuse their behavior, nor does it mean that we absolve them of wrong doing (p. 61–62; Romans 12:17–19).

- We must accept responsibility for our emotional reactions to offense rather than blame the offender (p. 64).

- Anger must be managed and eliminated in its negative expression (p. 70; Colossians 3:8; 3 Nephi 12:22).

- Patience and tolerance are important in anger management (p. 75; Hebrews 12:1).

- Rather than venting, we should stop angry thought and put our minds elsewhere (p. 78; Brigham Young, *Journal of Discourses,* 11:255).

- Whenever an issue is beyond our control, or when we won't care about it with the passage of time, it makes sense to decide that it doesn't matter—at least not enough to get upset about (p. 79; Matthew 6:34).

- When someone offends us, it's sometimes best to let it go, and other times it makes sense to confront the offender (p. 81; Matthew 18:15).

- It's healthy to confront an offender when we are moved upon by the Holy Ghost, but preferably if we do so soon after the offense, and only if we show an increase of love afterwards (p. 81; D&C 121:43).

- Fear (respect) of God is a useful emotion (p. 85; D&C 19:7; Luke 1:50).

- Those with faith in God need not fear (p. 86; 1 Timothy 1:7; D&C 10:55; Genesis 26:24).

- Being prepared temporally and spiritually is a great antidote against fear (p. 89; D&C 38:30).

- It isn't helpful to worry about what might happen in the future or to be over cautious or overly concerned about tomorrow (p. 90; Matthew 6:24).

- It's possible to turn our cares over to God (p. 91; 1 Peter 6:6–7; Psalm 54:22).

- Fear and faith are opposites. If we feed our faith, worry and fear will starve (p. 93; D&C 68:6; Jeremiah 17:7–8).

- Faith is built over time through ordinary means such as prayer, gospel study, service to others, and keeping the commandments (p. 93; Neal A. Maxwell, "Lest Ye Be Wearied and Faint in Your Minds," *Ensign,* May 1991, 88).

- In addition to faith in God's existence and in His love and mercy, we also need to know that our lives are moving in the right direction (p. 99; Joseph Smith, *Lectures on Faith* [Salt Lake City: Deseret Book, 1985], Lecture 6, Article 2).

- Self-esteem grows naturally when we practice charity and virtue in our lives (p. 103; D&C 121:45).

- Self-confidence grows naturally when we understand that we are children of God with an infinite potential (p. 104; Moses 1:4–13).

- Self-esteem requires more than self-affirmations. We must make correct choices over time (p. 105; Moses 6:31–37).

- The Atonement is a necessary ingredient in lasting self-esteem (p. 106; Isaiah 53:5; Alma 36:19–20).

- Once we have repented, we need not bring up or deal with our offenses in the future (p. 108; 2 Nephi 16:7; Isaiah 43:25).

- Procrastination, particularly putting off repentance, is one of the most costly mistakes we can make (p. 115; Helaman 13:38; Alma 13:27).

- In order to overcome the problem, those who procrastinate because they are pleasure seekers need a basic change in life philosophy (p. 118; D&C 84:38).

- For some people, basic organization skills are all that is needed to overcome procrastination (p. 120).

- Those who procrastinate for emotional reasons such as perfectionism, anger, or fear, must resolve those issues before they will have much luck overcoming procrastination (p. 121).

- Repentance cannot be put off without dire consequences (p. 128; Matthew 25:1–13; Alma 43:32–33).

- Sometimes changes we need to make in our lives are extremely difficult, but they are never impossible (p. 130; 1 Corinthians 10:13; 1 Nephi 3:7).

Concluding comment

As you know, life is designed as a test and a learning opportunity. Sailing is therefore guaranteed to be rough at times. We will all have our share of afflictions, but we are not left alone. The Lord said, "Be patient in afflictions, for thou shalt have many; but endure them, for, lo, I am with thee, even unto the end of thy days" (D&C 24:8). Along with the promise of having the Lord's Spirit with us, we also have an abundance of advice and counsel available from the Lord. This counsel comes to us directly as His words have been recorded by apostles and prophets. Apostles and prophets, under inspiration, have also put the truth in their own words.

My hope and prayer is that the brief review of these truths in this book will help each reader better cope with the normal and sometimes abnormal challenges of life. As you do so, your quality of life will improve. So will your ability to follow the counsel of the prophet Moroni, who at the very end of his ministry said:

> Yea, come unto Christ, and be perfected in him, and deny yourselves of all ungodliness; and if ye shall deny yourselves of all ungodliness, and love God with all your might, mind and strength, then is his grace sufficient for you, that by his grace ye may be perfect in Christ; and if by the grace of God ye are perfect in Christ, ye can in nowise deny the power of God. And again, if ye by the grace of God are perfect in Christ, and deny not his power, then are ye sanctified in Christ by the grace of God, through the shedding of the blood of Christ, which is in the covenant of the Father unto the remission of your sins, that ye become holy, without spot. (Moroni 10:32–33)

At that point, all emotional headaches will be a thing of the past. We will then have discovered the ultimate remedy for relief from all emotional and mental ills.

Notes
1. "Eternal Investments," address to religious educators, 10 Feb. 1989, 3.
2. Neal A. Maxwell, "Notwithstanding My Weakness," *Ensign*, Nov. 1976, 14.

About the author

GARY G. TAYLOR is a clinical psychologist who earned his PhD at Brigham Young University and taught at San Jose State University before entering private practice as a psychologist and family therapist. He has maintained a private practice for over thirty-five years in Northern California, Hawaii, and now South Jordan, Utah. Dr. Taylor has served as a counselor in several bishoprics and has also been a Gospel Doctrine Sunday School teacher and a high priests group leader in The Church of Jesus Christ of Latter-day Saints. He is the author of several books, two of which are currently available—*Sacred Union* and *The Perfect Parent*. Dr. Taylor and his wife, Melody, are the parents of ten and grandparents of twenty-one.